Promoting Happiness

Promoting Happiness

A workbook to help you appreciate
and get the most out of your life

Julia Barnard

MTC BOOKS

MTC Books
PO Box 268
St Agnes
SA 5097
Australia
books@makethechange.com.au

ISBN 978-0-9807590-0-6

Images by Leo Blanchette
Cover design by Pandelaide

http://www.promotinghappiness.com

To Andrew and my parents who support me in everything I do. Also to Kerry Cavanagh without whose motivation and gentle prompting this book would never have been completed.

Contents

Introduction

You are personally responsible for your own happiness. Every day you make a multitude of choices in your life and one of these is choosing to be happy. Of course, choosing happiness does not exempt you from the sad things that can happen in life. You will not get to the end of this workbook and suddenly life becomes perfect. Rather, you will have a better outlook on your past and present. You will also have a set of tools that you can use in your life that will aid you when you are up against it. Hopefully you will come to understand how much control you have in your life and realise how much is controlled by how you think about your world.

By working through this book, your happiness and wellbeing should have a boost, your overall outlook on life will be more positive and you will be better able to deal with stress.

The workbook is made up of clear sections that you can dip in and out of as you wish, although working through the whole book will help boost your awareness and happiness in many areas of your life. It makes sense to read Parts One and Two first. In particular, Part Two discusses faulty thinking which I refer to throughout. Being familiar with these ideas early on will be beneficial. As you progress through the book you will consider your past and present, to hopefully enable you to take yourself into a happier future. Each chapter includes activities for you to complete and tips that you can use in your everyday life. Some tips may speak to you more than others. When something inspires, hold on to it and use it as and when you can.

Using this workbook should be a pleasure and never to be a source of anxiety or worry. Have fun and enjoy the journey.

Part One: The Essentials

Part One introduces you to happiness. You will learn some very good reasons why you would want to promote happiness in your own life. See these as added bonuses for choosing to lead a happier, more fulfilled life.

Stress is a major problem for many people today and brings with it numerous health risks. As you embark on your happiness journey, you are doing what you can to cut down your stress and therefore the chances of developing a stress-related illness.

This section also introduces you to the activities that are a major part of this book. Such activities allow you to use what you learn to reflect on your own life. You will actually be applying ideas rather than just reading about them.

As I am sure you will gather as you proceed through this book, promoting happiness requires *you* to do the work. I offer you many tips and pointers, but it is down to you if you choose to use them.

The great thing about happiness is it becomes a cycle. By being happy, there are improvements in your life which serve to further increase happiness. It is a cycle that is worth being part of.

Chapter 1

REASONS TO BE HAPPY

Over the last ten years or so, research has provided us with some compelling reasons to be happy. Here is a brief rundown of some of the most interesting findings.[1]

Happy people:

- ❖ Have more successful marriages.

- ❖ Perform better in their jobs.

- ❖ Make better managers.

- ❖ Have fewer conflicts with their co-workers.

- ❖ Have greater job satisfaction.

- ❖ May have bigger incomes.

- ❖ Are more likely to help others.

- ❖ Have good, strong friendships.

- ❖ Have greater all-round satisfaction with life.

- ❖ Tend to make the most of their lives.

- ❖ Find enjoyment even in the most boring of tasks.

- ❖ Are better able to cope during difficult times.

---

[1] See: Lyubomirsky, S., King, L. A., & Diener, E. (2005) The Benefits of Frequent Positive Affect: Does Happiness Lead to Success? *Psychological Bulletin, 131,* 803-855.

Chapter 2

HEALTH BENEFITS OF HAPPINESS

Happiness can not only benefit you psychologically, it can also help keep you physically healthy. Below I have summarised some of the long term health benefits associated with happiness, positive thinking and optimism. [1]

❖ Optimism reduces your risk of dying from heart disease.

❖ Optimistic people may live longer.

❖ Laughter increases blood vessel function which can reduce the risk of cardiovascular disease.

❖ Overall physical health improves when you are optimistic about the future.

❖ An optimistic outlook reduces depression.

❖ Happiness reduces stress, which is a major cause of many health problems.

❖ Happy people have stronger immune systems and fewer illnesses.

❖ Optimism can lower cortisol levels – a hormone associated with stress and ill-health.

❖ The happier you are, the less likely you are to have hypertension.

❖ Happy people are less likely to suffer from burnout.

---

[1] Research support found in Appendix 1

Chapter 3

JOURNAL WRITING

As you proceed through this workbook you will have many opportunities to write and reflect. Although space is provided, I strongly recommend you get yourself a journal. Some activities are ongoing and a journal is a good place to put them. It can just be a cheap notebook which you personalise. Remember, the focus is on promoting happiness, so keep your journal relevant to this.

You may want to date your entries so you can keep track of your happiness progress. If you find you want to journal issues and concerns that are not particularly positive but you know you would benefit from writing down, set up a separate journal.

The following icons have been used in this book:

When you see this icon, it is to indicate you should use your journal to expand on the work being done in this book.

This indicates an activity, where you will get to apply the ideas you are reading about. Don't be afraid to write on your book. It has been designed for this purpose.

TIP Many tips are found throughout the workbook. They are hints and ideas to help you get the most from your happiness journey.

Chapter 4

DEFINE HAPPINESS

How would you define happiness? This is your first activity and since happiness is a personal thing, so should be your definition.

I would like to point out however what happiness is *not*. It is not about being liked, famous, or wealthy. It is not about having more stuff. Materialism is likely to make you unhappy. Also, importantly, happiness is not the end of bad things and low moods. Life affects happy people as much as anybody else (the difference is how they cope).

In the space below, write your definition of happiness. As you proceed through this workbook you may find your definition changes or you get new ideas. Keep adding to your list, or use your journal.

_____

_____

_____

_____

_____

_____

_____

_____

_____

_____

Chapter 5

INITIAL HAPPINESS EVALUATION

How happy are you today? How happy are you with your past? How optimistic are you about the future? You can rate your happiness out of 10 or describe how you feel more fully. You may want to use your journal to reflect further. If you are feeling creative, you may want to do a drawing in the space below.

_____

_____

_____

_____

_____

_____

_____

_____

_____

Get creative here

Part Two: Understand Your Thinking Patterns

What follows is a brief guide to identifying your patterns of thought and how you can change them, if needed. It will help you understand just how much an impact your thoughts can make on your happiness and your life overall.

It is worth familiarising yourself with this part, because I refer back to these ideas throughout the book. If you can make headway in identifying and overcoming unrealistic thoughts, you are setting yourself up for a happier life.

For a more comprehensive account you might read books by Albert Ellis. In particular, his book 'A Guide to Rational Living' or 'How to Stubbornly Refuse to Make Yourself Miserable About Anything – Yes Anything'.

Chapter 6

THE IMPORTANCE OF YOUR THOUGHTS

Your thoughts are very powerful and should not be underestimated. They will impact on how you interpret your past, deal with your present and consider your future. They can make the difference between a happy life and a miserable one. Your thinking is not always sensible, logical or even realistic. It is these thoughts that cause so much unhappiness. They can however be challenged and replaced with more realistic thinking.

The activities that follow are designed to increase your awareness of your own thought patterns. Being aware of your thoughts puts you in a position to do something about them. They may be ones you have accepted for many, many years. Yet it is possible to make changes. The ideal outcome is to work towards having thoughts which are rational, realistic, flexible and positive.

I will begin by introducing you to faulty thinking and some common errors of thinking that people make. You will then carry out a thought recording exercise where you will spend time tuning into your own faulty thinking patterns when faced with certain situations.

You will move on to identifying what happens as a result of the thoughts you have. In other words, what are the consequences of your thoughts? This is crucial. It is your thoughts that determine what happens next, not the situation itself. Having identified your faulty thinking patterns, you will work on challenging them and replacing them with more realistic thoughts.

Hopefully, with your new, realistic thoughts, you will come to see some positive outcomes that will help you lead a happier life.

Recognising faulty thinking

As I said at the start of this chapter, your thoughts are not always sensible or logical. The trouble is, when your thoughts are not always rational, they can get in the way of you having a happy life. If you can identify faulty thoughts you have, then you are in a good position to change them and your life.

Faulty thinking appears in a number of different guises. Have a look at the following list. These are all types of faulty thinking. Take the time to reflect on them. Some you may instantly recognise in yourself, others you may have without even realising it. You may like to put a cross next to those thoughts familiar to you. Also, as you read them, think about why they are faulty.

COMMON TYPES OF FAULTY THINKING

Using words such as 'must', 'ought', 'should', 'have to'.
e.g. "I should always win".

Making statements that include the words 'never' or 'always'.
e.g. "This always happens to me".

Minimising the positive.
e.g. "Oh I was just lucky".

Maximising the negative.
e.g. "Nothing good happened today".

Expecting the worst to happen.
e.g. "We'll lose our home".

Striving for perfectionism.
e.g. "I must not make a mistake".

Taking things personally.
e.g. "She ignored me just then, I obviously did something to offend her".

Underestimating the control you have in your life.
e.g. "My past was awful, so I can never be happy".

Assuming control when there is none.
e.g. "He can't say that to me".

Thought recording

As you go through your day you will find yourself confronted with particular situations or scenarios, both good and bad. It could be an upcoming activity, an argument, disappointment, failure to meet a goal or something new happening in your life. You may be feeling stressed or unhappy.

 **Write down the situation, scenario or event that happened.** You will probably want to use your journal as you continue with this activity for other situations.

e.g. *Going to a party Saturday night.*

_____

_____

_____

_____

_____

_____

_____

_____

Identify your thoughts and beliefs. What do you say to yourself about the situation? **This is where you will begin to identify your faulty thinking.**

e.g. *Nobody will speak to me. I'll have nothing to talk about.*

_____

_____

_____

_____

_____

_____

_____

Having identified your thoughts, you need to become aware of what happens next. What do you do, what do you say, how do you feel? What are your physical symptoms?

e.g. *Maybe I should cancel, I feel sick, I can't sleep with worry.*

_____

_____

_____

_____

_____

In the above activity, you have just identified the consequences of your thoughts. So in the example, the party in itself was not the problem. The problem was in believing nobody would speak to them, which led to feelings of sickness, sleep problems and thinking about not going.

16

With time hopefully you will come to recognise that it is your thoughts and beliefs that lead to these consequences, not the situation itself. Remember it is not the event itself that causes a behavioural response; it is how we think about the event that leads to certain behaviours.

Challenge your thinking

Now you will begin to challenge the faulty thoughts you have identified above. By challenging your thinking, you are in a position to change them and develop new and more realistic thoughts. Learning to dispute your unhelpful thinking will help you to carry on despite setbacks and to acknowledge your abilities and the role *you* play in *your* life. This may take work, but with practise it can become a natural skill which you can use every day.

Take a look at some of the faulty thoughts you have already identified. For each one, consider the following questions:

1. Where is the firm evidence that what I am thinking is true?

2. Is my thinking all or nothing?

3. Am I disregarding my strengths and focusing on my weaknesses?

4. Am I blaming myself or other people unnecessarily? Consider all the factors that may have contributed to the situation.

5. Am I demanding perfection?

6. Am I exaggerating the importance of certain things?

7. Am I assuming the situation is totally out of my control?

8. Is the outcome realistically going to be so awful?

9. Does my thinking make logical sense?

10. Where is holding on to the belief getting me?

Can you identify faulty thinking? Note down what you learn about your thoughts here.

e.g. My thinking is all or nothing. I am assuming I will have no control. My thoughts are causing me to feel quite ill and are unhelpful.

_____

_____

_____

_____

_____

_____

_____

_____

_____

_____

_____

_____

_____

_____

Now challenge your thoughts. Write down what is really true and logical about the situation.

e.g. It is unlikely nobody will speak to me and I am in
reality capable of making conversation. 'Nothing' is an
extreme thing to say and is all or nothing thinking.

_____

_____

_____

_____

_____

_____

_____

_____

_____

_____

By challenging your thoughts, change can begin, as you are questioning thoughts that may have been with you for a long time.

New beliefs

Having challenged your old beliefs, you will want to replace them with more realistic beliefs. These new beliefs you will practise saying to yourself as you get used to challenging your old beliefs. Remember, chances are your faulty beliefs have been with you for some time and have been taken for granted. Like learning anything new, it can take a while before your new beliefs become comfortable and automatic.

Replace your old unrealistic belief with a new, more rational belief.

Old belief	New belief
e.g. Nobody will speak to me	Somebody will speak to me. Natalie is the host and she will speak to me. I will get her to introduce me to some people. If nobody speaks to me, it is not the end of the world.

New consequences

As you take on your new beliefs, you will see your situation in a more realistic light. What follows from this are a new set of responses, both behavioural and emotional. Rather than feeling stressed and unhappy, you will be better able to manage the situation. Importantly you will feel more in control and understand the impact your thoughts have on your life and happiness levels.

Note down the positive outcomes of your new beliefs. Consider your behaviour and emotions as well as any other benefits that happen. You may want to come back to this activity as you come to recognise the different benefits your new thoughts bring.

e.g. I am looking forward to the party. I will chat to people I do know, I will read the paper beforehand so I have something interesting to talk about if talk doesn't come easily. I finally got some sleep last night.

Support for your new beliefs

For maximum benefit, you will want to test out the new beliefs that you have worked so hard at creating. You will need to prove them right and there is no better way than through action. This can take courage, but if you persevere you really will see how your thinking can change your life. So with the example, I would go to the party, taking my realistic thoughts with me.

As you gain support for your new beliefs, they will become part of your life and will replace those old, unhelpful beliefs that caused you unhappiness.

How are you going to support your new beliefs? Give as much detail as possible, noting when, where and how it will happen. You can also note the outcomes of what you did here.

e.g. I will go to the party. I will arrive at 8pm. I will go speak to
Natalie and get her to introduce me to some people. The party
was great. I chatted to a few people and felt quite relaxed. I
wasn't exactly the life and soul, but that's not me anyway.
I was happy and in my comfort zone.

TIP The activities you worked through in this chapter you can repeat as often as needed. Keep identifying your faulty thought patterns, question and challenge them and replace them with more realistic beliefs.

Part Three: A Happy Past

You cannot change your past. However, you can change how you think about your past. Sometimes it is easy to get so caught up in the past that it is preventing happiness in the present. Reflecting on the past may leave you feeling bitter or resentful. Past experiences have left you unhappy and unable to enjoy your present or have any hope for the future. It is easy to come to believe that there was absolutely nothing good in your past. This section is an opportunity to reset the balance.

Some of these activities may be a challenge for you. You may wonder why you should think about the good, when so much bad has happened. Remember, it is you that is suffering from your thoughts. Having the courage to rethink your life can make living with yourself a pleasure.

Chapter 7

REBALANCING YOUR LIFE

You will need your journal for this chapter, since it can be regarded as an ongoing project. Put simply, you are going to attempt to review your life, so you can learn a more balanced account of your past. It is an opportunity to help you realise that the misfortunes in your past were not all that your past was about. You may be used to using your unhappy past to explain who you are today. However, it is not just the bad things that make up the complexity that is you. History is not written in stone and is always open to reinterpretation.

With reflection and a great deal of introspection and courage you can work towards a more balanced account of your past. It will probably take time and you may struggle. Recognise that this activity is for you and taking control of your life is very empowering. You will free up your thoughts, allowing you to enjoy your present and look forward to your future. By rebalancing your life you will come to see that your past was not all bad and it is not fair to yourself to hold onto just the bad.

In your rewrite you want to focus on the positive things that happened in your life. The enjoyable times, times of achievement and excitement. Reflect on the people that were there for you. Consider the strengths you displayed. You may need to train your mind to stop you from wandering back to the difficult times. This may take determination if such thinking has become automatic for you.

You can carry out this task any way you like. You can work a year at a time, working backwards or forwards to the present day. Or you may want to focus on major events in your life or begin with smaller things from your past.

The following activities and tips are intended to help you reflect on your past and assist you with your rebalance. They can however be used in their own right, so feel free to pick and choose activities that work for you. Remember to use your journal if you run out of space.

Note one fond memory for every year of your life, going back as far as you can remember.

_____
_____
_____
_____
_____
_____
_____
_____
_____
_____
_____
_____
_____
_____
_____
_____

Take a large sheet of paper. In very small writing in the bottom right corner, write out the unhappy event from your past that has stayed with you. Then use the rest of the paper to write out all the good things that happened during that time. Take as long as you like and try to fill the page.

TIP When reflecting on negative events, you may need to tune into your thinking patterns. Be alert to faulty thinking and dispute it as often as possible. Make a note of your insights as you are freed up from your former thoughts and more realistic and helpful thoughts evolve.

Remember that 'nothing' is an example of faulty thinking. Your life is made up of a multitude of events, so you are being hard on yourself if you find yourself declaring that nothing good happened in your past. TIP

Using imagery can help you get in touch with your positive emotions. Begin by recalling your happiest childhood memory. Now sit back, close your eyes and relax. Imagine that memory as vividly as you can, conjuring up the thoughts and feelings you experienced back then. Note down how you felt afterwards.

_____

_____

_____

_____

_____

_____

_____

_____

_____

_____

_____

Recall your best friend from childhood and some of the things you did together and the good times you shared. Write some of your recollections here.

_____

_____

_____

_____

_____

_____

_____

_____

What did you love about school? List all your fond memories, taking the time to recall the good feelings associated with those memories.

_____

_____

_____

_____

_____

_____

_____

_____

_____

_____

Can you recall any interesting neighbours or people in your community that made you laugh or smile? Are there any particular experiences which stand out?

_____

_____

_____

_____

_____

_____

_____

_____

_____

_____

_____

_____

_____

One way of rethinking your childhood is through an understanding of the transactional model of child development[1]. Simply put, this model states that a child plays an important, active role in their social development. As such the child's actions have an impact on the parent, who in turn impacts on the child.

If this model is true, is it possible that you can reinterpret your past as something you were an active part of rather than something that simply happened to you?

---

[1] To learn more about this model, you may like to read 'The Transactional Model of Development: How Children and Contexts Shape Each Other'. Edited by Arnold Sameroff, published 2009 by APA.

Think about your personal strengths. What strengths did you find yourself displaying earlier on in life? What strengths are you proud to exhibit today which have evolved from your handling of past events?

_____

_____

_____

_____

_____

_____

_____

_____

_____

_____

Think about the time when you were most down and your mood was at an all-time low. What did you do to set yourself on your feet again? What things would you use again?

_____

_____

_____

_____

_____

_____

_____

We often use certain words to describe the type of person that we are. Some of these labels we may have adopted from the words of others and may not be altogether helpful, positive or for that matter realistic. Starting today, do away with the negative labels attributed to you as a child. Dispute them each and every day until you realise they are invalid. Deliberately carry out behaviours that prove the labels false.

This chapter has been about rebalancing. Its aim is to remind you that your life is not *all* bad. My intention is not to deny that difficult times happened. Rather, it is an attempt to remind you that your past is made up of good as well as bad events.

Chapter 8

REGRETS

As you reflect on your past, you may recall certain events with regret. You need to recognise that you cannot physically change the past, but you *can* change how you think about it. Holding on to regrets can keep you unhappy and have the potential to blot out the possibility of a better future. You may be blinkered to the good things that are and could be in your life. Dealing with your regrets may help you with your rebalancing work in the previous chapter.

TIP Remember to keep a look out for faulty thinking as you reflect on your regrets. Look out for statements like 'should have', or unreasonable self-blame. Refer to Part Two if you need help with this.

List as many reasons as you can think of to support the statement **"it is pointless having regrets"**.

_____

_____

_____

_____

_____

_____

_____

_____

_____

_____

TIP If you are still holding on to regretful feelings from your past, try setting up a ritual to help you deal with it. For example, write out your regret and then throw it away.

If you have a regret that still nags at you, try the following activity. Write down your regret. Then say to yourself, **"if I had followed this path, I would have missed out on the following..."** Now note the people you met, the things you have done and all the positive things associated with what you did do instead.

_____

_____

_____

_____

_____

_____

_____

_____

_____

_____

_____

_____

_____

_____

TIP Remember you cannot know how your life would have been if you had taken a different course; that's what makes life so exciting.

TIP Don't assume if you had chosen a different path you would have lived happily ever after and your life would be perfect. Research[1] has shown that people expect to feel good for a lot longer when they experience positive events than they actually do.

Make sure there are no regrets in your future. If you were to live your life as you are currently, would you have any regrets years down the line? If so, write them down and think about the steps you can take to make the changes that would prevent those potential regrets from becoming a reality. You will then want to put these steps into action. I discuss setting and achieving goals in a later chapter.

_____

_____

_____

_____

_____

_____

_____

_____

_____

_____

_____

_____

[1] See: Wilson, T.D. & Gilbert, D.T. (2005) Affective forecasting: Knowing What to Want. *Current Directions in Psychological Science* Vol 14 No 3 pp131-134.
You may also like to read Dan Gilbert's book: Stumbling on Happiness.

Chapter 9

FORGIVENESS

People let you down; they cause you anger and disappointment. Working towards happiness cannot prevent this happening. However, if you are unable to move on and forgive that person, it is you that is left feeling miserable and unhappy. Every time you reflect on the event you feel the injustice and this is doing nothing for your wellbeing. It may even be preventing you from successfully working through the rebalancing activity discussed earlier. If you can forgive, you will be able to move on with your life and free yourself from bitterness.

Detail events in your life that you are struggling to forgive. Think about things you have been holding on to for a long time as well as smaller situations that you are unwilling to let go.

_____

_____

_____

_____

_____

_____

_____

_____

_____

_____

_____

_____

_____

What is standing in the way of you being able to forgive? Allow time to reflect on this activity and write down what comes to you.

_____

_____

_____

_____

_____

_____

_____

_____

How might faulty thinking be contributing to this? Do you find yourself saying 'why should I?' or 'I can't do that'? Think of new statements that challenge these thoughts. Refer to the faulty thinking section in Part Two if necessary.

_____

_____

_____

_____

_____

_____

_____

_____

_____

Why it is important to forgive

If you are able to forgive, you will have reduced stress and anger, increased optimism and better health. Research[1] indicates that unforgiving people tend to have higher heart rates and blood pressure and more negative emotions.

Walking around with unforgiving thoughts becomes a burden to you and you alone. The perpetrator may have no idea how you feel – they are getting on with their life and at the same time your thoughts are hindering you from getting on with yours. In a sense, the power remains with them.

By forgiving another, you are able to resume control. You are not giving in or condoning their actions; rather you are allowing yourself to get on with your life.

How do you think forgiving will benefit you personally?

_____

_____

_____

_____

_____

_____

_____

_____

_____

_____

[1] See: Witvliet, C.V., Ludwig, T.E., & Vander, K.L. (2001). Granting forgiveness or harbouring grudges: Implications for emotion, physiology and health. *Psychological Science*, 12, 117-123.

Forgiveness is not just about past events. It is something worth practising in your daily life. Try to forgive quickly before the situation is made more complicated and becomes a long running battle that dominates your life.

How to forgive

Work through the following activities to assist you in learning how to forgive. Remember to use your journal to expand on the thoughts and feelings you have as you complete each step.

If you find yourself getting upset, carry out a relaxation exercise. Try breathing in slowly through your nose then out through your mouth, until you feel calm again.

In the first activity in this chapter, you listed things you were struggling to forgive. **Choose one event that you would like to forgive** and note it here.

_____

_____

_____

_____

_____

_____

How you are thinking and feeling right now about the situation and the person you would like to forgive?

_____

_____

_____

_____

_____

_____

Spend time recalling the event, but now be as objective as possible. How would an outsider view the situation? Try not to feel sorry for yourself.

_____

_____

_____

_____

_____

_____

_____

Make a deliberate choice to forgive. Tell yourself that you have chosen to forgive and it is done freely and without a grudge.

_____

_____

_____

_____

_____

Now write down the reasons why you have made the decision to forgive.

_____

_____

_____

_____

_____

_____

Imagine you are the person you want to forgive. Try to understand their point of view. Try to feel empathy and tune into their weaknesses. Reflect on why they may have hurt you in the first place.

_____

_____

_____

_____

_____

_____

_____

_____

For forgiveness to be effective you need to take action. Decide what physical thing you are going to do to acknowledge your forgiveness of the other person. You could put it in a letter, write it in your journal, or perhaps tell a friend. You do not have to do it face to face, since forgiveness is for your benefit. Work out the details of when, where and who will be involved.

_____

_____

_____

_____

_____

_____

_____

_____

_____

_____

TIP A creative way to forgive is to design a Certificate of Forgiveness. In Iris Murdoch's novel 'The Sea, The Sea', the main character talks of a Certificate of Forgiveness. Design your own Certificate of Forgiveness, recording names and details of what you are forgiving. Spend time making it look attractive, with colours and interesting fonts. As with any certificate, remember to date it.

How are you feeling now? What new feelings do you have? Reflect on how it feels to let go of a grudge. Consider the benefits to you and the people around you.

_____

_____

_____

_____

_____

_____

_____

_____

TIP If necessary, remind yourself on a regular basis that you have forgiven the person, so you can move on with your life.

Repeat the section 'How to Forgive' as often as needed, as you work through different events in your life.

Chapter 10

PAST SUCCESSES AND ACHIEVEMENTS

We often underestimate how much we've achieved both in the distant and more immediate past. This chapter is all about these successes. It is an opportunity to recall different events in your life, which you can take with you as you continue on in the world. Hopefully you will come to appreciate how much control you have had over the things that you have accomplished so far. Remember, a happy outlook may help you be more successful in the future. Watch your success list just grow and grow.

This chapter is not just about those huge things you have achieved. It is the small things also. It is about personal conquests and triumphs, as well as all the things you are proud of. It can include those things reached through a lot of hard work, effort and determination. It can be persevering in the face of prejudice or scepticism, or a seemingly impossible obstacle. Think also about your personal battles (perhaps only you know about them) and how you conquered them. Confronting your own emotions, changing a behaviour, breaking a habit – these are all wonderful successes.

As you work through this section, reflect on what these things tell you about the sort of person you are. You may come to understand a bit more about the things you value and what matters in your life.

TIP When completing these activities do not fall into the trap of faulty thinking: 'I have achieved nothing', 'other people have done more than me', 'I was just lucky'.

What is the earliest success you can remember? Write down as many details as possible that you can recall.

_____

_____

_____

_____

_____

_____

_____

_____

Recall some of the successes you have had to date in relation to your home life. You may like to consider your personal relationships, your family and your friendships.

_____

_____

_____

_____

_____

_____

_____

_____

_____

_____

_____

Think about your working life. Note down some of your achievements. Such achievements may have been for you personally as well as ones that came to have a positive impact in the life of others (think about colleagues and customers).

_____

_____

_____

_____

_____

_____

_____

_____

_____

_____

Reflect on your educational achievements. This does not have to just be qualifications earned, but any learning experiences you are particularly proud of.

_____

_____

_____

_____

_____

_____

_____

_____

_____

Think about your community. List your successes and accomplishments. Think of voluntary work as well as activities in your neighbourhood, your church, contributions to charity, or events at your child's school. How did your actions benefit others?

_____

_____

_____

_____

_____

_____

_____

TIP When completing these activities remember to focus on what you are personally proud of. Don't go comparing yourself to others or dismiss something because it seems insignificant.

Reflect on those successes met in your leisure time. Think of the accomplishments made through your sports or hobbies. Remember these can be personal goals as well as public achievements.

_____

_____

_____

_____

_____

_____

_____

List difficult things in your past that you have overcome, ultimately bringing a good result for you.

_____

_____

_____

_____

_____

_____

_____

_____

_____

_____

List the things you achieved just last week. Remember an achievement does not have to be life changing to be deemed a success. It can be anything that had a positive impact on your life or the life of another.

_____

_____

_____

_____

_____

_____

_____

_____

_____

_____

TIP Take time to recapture how you felt at the time of your success. Such emotions do not last forever and normality soon resumes. Reflecting on them now will remind you how much that goal meant to you and will enable you to relive those good emotions.

What one thing are you most proud of?

_____

_____

_____

_____

_____

_____

Looking back on the successes you have listed, what skills and strengths did you draw upon to make these a reality?

_____

_____

_____

_____

_____

_____

_____

_____

_____

How might you use these strengths today to ensure you have more success in the future?

_____

_____

_____

_____

_____

_____

_____

_____

Part Four: Here, Now and Onwards

Hopefully you now have a better insight into your past. You are aware of your successes, can stop winding yourself up about regrets and are ready to enjoy your life as it is today.

Enjoying the here and now is an important part of bringing about greater happiness in your life. However, the here and now will always bring challenges. This section is therefore dedicated to helping you making the most of your life.

Be aware, promoting happiness in your life does not mean the end of tricky times. Rather, it will help you bring about a shift in perspective so you can better handle the difficult patches and make the most of the good times. This will also help you move onwards into a future you cannot predict but will hopefully have the mental strength to handle well.

Enjoy each chapter and remember to have fun. It's about getting the most out of you and your life.

Chapter 11

SUPPORT

As you go through life and face different challenges, the task can be made a whole lot easier with the support and help of other people.

Support can be given for different reasons and can come from a number of sources. For example, a family member who helped to fix your plumbing or a friend who will listen to your relationship problems are both sources of support. Other people in your life can offer help, advice, encouragement and offer positive feedback.

Why is support so important? It can be good for your mental and physical health. There has been research[1] that suggests the more connections a person had the less likely they were to die. Recent research published in the American Journal of Public Health[2] showed that memory decline in older people was less when they had more social ties. The support from others can help you deal with stress which can have a great impact on your long term health. Furthermore it may reduce loneliness and boost self-esteem.

The following will help you consider the support you have in different areas of your life. Hopefully the activities will increase your awareness of the support you do have, and to recognise how support benefits you.

---

[1] See: Berkman, L.S. & Syme, S.L. (1978) Social networks, host resistance and mortality, *American Journal of Epidemiology,* 109, pp186-204.
[2] Ertel, K.A., Glymour, M.M., & Berkman, L.F. (2008) Effects of social integration on preserving memory function in a nationally representative U.S. elderly population, *American Journal of Public Health,* Vol. 98, No. 7.

TIP When considering support think of those people who offer you practical as well as emotional assistance.

Identify family members you can receive support from as well as the nature of this support. Think of your extended family as well as your more immediate relatives.

_____

_____

_____

_____

_____

_____

_____

_____

Identify any family members whose support you have not used in the last six months yet you could probably draw upon if needed.

_____

_____

_____

_____

_____

_____

_____

_____

Research[1] has shown that when women were in difficult, stressful circumstances, those with a close, supportive husband were less likely to develop depression compared to women without such support. Having a close friend to talk to also helped. Friendship can boost mood, increase self-esteem as well as ease stress and worries. Friends can help reduce isolation, boredom and loneliness.

What sort of support does your partner offer you?

_____

_____

_____

_____

_____

_____

List your friends and the different ways they support you. Remember your friends do not have to live close to you to be a source of support and you may have friends you have met online.

_____

_____

_____

_____

_____

_____

_____

[1] See: Brown, G.W. & Harris, T. (1978) *Social Origins of Depression*, London, Tavistock.

TIP Schedule a regular time to meet up with your friends. If this is not possible, email them, send a card or write them a letter.

A great chunk of time is spent at work and indeed it can be a very stressful place. As such, having support from colleagues is important. They can help you deal with a difficult boss, a tricky client or the general day to day issues unique to your workplace.

Who at work offers you support? Consider not only the people who you can turn to when you want to unburden but those who offer you more practical assistance when needed. Note how each person is important to you.

Support can also come from professional groups. For example, your doctor, social workers, counsellors and/or support groups. These sources can offer information and advice as well as emotional support.

What professional support do you have in your life? Consider how frequently you use them and for what purpose.

_____

_____

_____

_____

_____

_____

If you were struggling with an issue and unable to find a resolution, would you see a counsellor? Give your reasons. How might a counsellor help?

_____

_____

_____

_____

_____

What support does your local community offer? Consider your neighbours, your church as well as community services available to you. Try to give specific examples of how your community has supported you over the years.

_____

_____

_____

_____

_____

_____

Another source of support available is information. This can come from books, journals, websites, magazines, and so on. The support can be both practical and emotional. For instance, there are many forums available on the web that offer users support from people they have never met. Books and magazines can offer practical tips as well as self-help guides for coping.

How do you use the internet and books to obtain support? Do you have different sources of information support for your work life and your home life?

_____

_____

_____

_____

_____

_____

_____

_____

Remember, support does not just have to come from other people. Your own personal resources can be a great means of support. For example, consider your qualities and strengths, coping strategies that you know work, as well as your accumulation of past experiences.

How do you support yourself during difficult times? Brainstorm new things you could try to help you cope in the future.

_____

_____

_____

_____

_____

_____

_____

Review the above activities where you have identified your sources of support. Identify areas in your life where you are under-supported. How might you change this? Is faulty thinking getting in the way?

_____

_____

_____

_____

_____

_____

_____

TIP This chapter has been about the support you receive. You may like to also reflect on how you support other people both at work and home.

Chapter 12

SELF-ACCEPTANCE

If you want a happier life, it is important that you accept who you are. This includes being proud of your good things, acknowledging your flaws without undue criticism and generally being able to appreciate your own company. It is about being at ease with yourself.

The following activities are aimed at increasing your satisfaction with who you are. You will spend time exploring what you like about yourself and trying to bring about some acceptance of the person you are today.

Answer the following: 'what do I love about being me?' Add to your list as you progress through the book.

_____

_____

_____

_____

_____

_____

_____

_____

_____

To feel good about yourself, it is important that you like yourself. If there are things that you do not like about yourself, it is important that you accept them as part of the wonderfully complex character that is you.

As part of being me, I accept:

_____

_____

_____

_____

_____

_____

_____

_____

_____

TIP Try not to compare yourself to others. This includes people you know as well as people you see on TV or in magazines. Do what feels right for you and you alone. With media messages telling us how to look and act, including important life decisions, remember they are not speaking specifically to you. Do not feel judged by something that changes in the same way fashion does.

Identify the varied roles you perform in your life and what you enjoy most about each of them.

_____

_____

_____

_____

_____

_____

_____

Focusing on the good things in your life, rather than the bad, will give you a boost and help you feel better about yourself.

TIP

Identify your strengths. Strengths can refer to your character strengths, as well as things you are good at.

_____

_____

_____

_____

_____

_____

_____

_____

_____

_____

If you visit the Authentic Happiness website[1] you can complete the VIA Signature Strengths questionnaire. It will identify your top strengths. Take the time to look at these strengths and reflect on them. Increasing research[2] shows using your strengths can increase wellbeing and happiness. What steps can you take to use your strengths in your daily life?

---

[1] www.authentichappiness.org
[2] See for example: Seligman, M.E.P., Steen, T.A., Park, N. & Peterson, C. (2005) Positive Psychology progress: empirical validation of interventions, _American Psychologist,_ Vol 60, No 5 pp410-421.

How satisfied are you with different areas of your life? Consider areas that are important to you. For example you may want to consider relationships, work, home and leisure. Rate them on a scale of 1 to 10, 1 being extremely unsatisfied and 10 being extremely satisfied.

Area of your life	Satisfaction Rating

What changes might you make so that when you ask this question again in a year, you have moved up the satisfaction scale (say from a 5 to a 7)?

TIP When things go wrong, recognise that it does not undermine the essence of who you are. If you made a mistake, work to correct it (if this is feasible) then move on. Hold yourself in high regard.

Body image

When we speak of self, let's not forget our bodies. How we think about our bodies can have a massive impact on our self-esteem, confidence and ultimately our happiness.

Are you a fan of your body, or are you striving to be thinner? Do you believe thin equals happy? I have read a lot of happiness research and I am yet to come across any that says being thin is the key to happiness.

However, there is research[1] that has shown women who saw images of young, flawless models went on to rate their own bodies more negatively and their depression levels increased. Remember such images aren't real. Even novices can touch up a digital photo, so imagine what the experts can do?

What are the favourite parts of your body?

_____

_____

_____

_____

[1] Hamilton, E.A., Mintz, L. & Kashubeck-West, S. (2007) Predictors of media effects on body dissatisfaction in European American women, *Sex Roles: A Journal of Research, Vol 56, No 5-6,* pp397-402.

If you like your body you are more likely to look after it. As such, you will exercise regularly and eat well. You don't worry about diets which are a constant reminder of the dissatisfaction you have with your body. Furthermore, exercise can help you appreciate how amazing your body is and what it is capable of. It also brings many benefits. The chapters on exercise and food expand more on these ideas.

What activities do you do to look after your body on a daily basis?

_____

_____

_____

_____

_____

What activities are you _not_ currently doing, which you would like to do, to ensure you look after your body? For each activity, note when you are going to carry them out. Activities can be anything positive, for example, limiting take away food, reading health magazines, walking more, taking your doctor's advice.

_____

_____

_____

_____

_____

_____

Look at yourself in a full-length mirror. Appreciate what you see without criticism. Note your reflections here (no pun intended, however when I re-read this, I had to leave it in!).

_____

_____

_____

_____

_____

_____

_____

Starting now, forget about negative comments anyone | TIP | has ever made about your body. They do not define you. Rather, what you say to yourself does.

How does faulty thinking get in the way of you accepting your body? When thinking about your body, carry out the faulty thinking exercises outlined in Part Two. In particular, note how often you say to yourself "I must". Record your findings here.

_____

_____

_____

_____

_____

_____

_____

_____

_____

Make a conscious choice over the programmes you
watch and the magazines you read. For example 'How
to Look Good Naked' has to be more uplifting than
those that promote surgery as part of a makeover.

TIP

TIP Appreciate all the things your body does. Read a book
on biology if you want to know more about how
amazing your body is.

Being alone

Being happy with yourself enables you to enjoy your own
company. You can feel comfortable and secure without
looking to other people for your entertainment. Try to spend
time each week doing activities alone.

**What activities do you enjoy pursuing by
yourself?** You may want to include past activities
that you have not done for a while, but enjoy doing.

_____

_____

_____

_____

_____

_____

_____

_____

_____

Chapter 13

WORK SATISFACTION

A great deal of time is spent at work, so it's worth trying to get the most out of it. Work is one place where you are often faced with things you cannot change: policies you find senseless, a thoughtless manager, a gloomy workspace. To get more satisfaction from work it is important to be able to focus on the things you *can* change – namely your thoughts, feelings, attitudes and behaviours. How you approach work can make a huge difference to your life.

The following activities offer opportunities for you to reflect on your work and devise and implement strategies to get the most out of your day. Remember to keep a look out for faulty thinking, which may be impacting on your work satisfaction.

List current likes and dislikes you have about work. Be specific so you know exactly which things you do and do not enjoy.

Likes	Dislikes

Use your journal to help you work through the following four steps.

1. Look at your dislikes list. For each dislike, brainstorm as many ideas as possible for how you can make the situation better or at least more bearable for yourself. Really get creative and don't rule out any idea you have.

2. For each idea, go through and rate the advantages and disadvantages of each.

3. From this you should be able to agree a solution that is workable for you. Be aware that you cannot change what other people think, say or do. Happily you can change and control what *you* think, say or do. I talk more about change in a later chapter.

4. Remember to carry out your solution!

TIP Don't assume your boss knows what you want from your work. It's easy to sit quietly, hoping for change. Arrange a time to talk to them about what you want and how you want to bring it about. They may not be able to help you, but at least you took control, rather than just wishing and wondering.

Any job can be made to feel more meaningful given some creative thinking. Set goals and challenges that you can achieve at work on a daily or weekly basis. These can be for your own purpose or ones that will help you achieve a deadline you have been set.

Brainstorm some goals and challenges that you could implement into your working day.

_____

_____

_____

_____

_____

_____

_____

How might you personally make the workplace a happier place for yourself and others? Remember, small changes can make all the difference.

_____

_____

_____

_____

_____

_____

TIP If you have your own desk, office or workspace, do what you can to personalise it.

You know your job is important right? If it wasn't, it wouldn't exist. As such, try to get the most out of each day, rather than living for the future. Feel good about what you do and how it contributes to the organisation you work for, as well as society as a whole.

How does your work make a difference to the lives of others?

_____

_____

_____

_____

_____

_____

_____

_____

_____

_____

For one week, keep a record of five good things that happened at work each day. Then reflect on what you are looking forward to the next day.

TIP   It's nice to be praised for the work you do. Sadly, it doesn't always happen. A solution is to praise yourself when you know you have done a good job and reward yourself when you've met particular goals or deadlines.

TIP   When considering a promotion, ask yourself how it will benefit your happiness. Be honest in weighing up the pros and cons of going for a potential promotion. Remember that money alone won't bring happiness.

Colleagues

You spend a great deal of time with your colleagues. They can be a source of support and laughter, especially when you are working together to meet deadlines. However, it's often all too easy to ignore each other or only focus on the things that you find annoying about them. As such, try to pass the time of day with your co-workers. You never know who may become a friend.

TIP Don't be the one that comments on other people's behaviour. You know the sort of thing: the time they get in, the time they leave, how long they took for lunch, what they wear. It annoys you so it is sure to annoy them. Instead, focus on what is going on for you. Be secure enough to not have to worry about the schedules of others.

TIP Try not to compare yourself with others. This applies in other areas of life but can be a particular issue at work. Look at your own needs and what you want to achieve from your work.

Work / life balance

It is important to have a balance in your life. I have written a separate chapter on relaxation which is worth reading to ensure you take time out to reduce stress.

TIP Do something non-work related with your lunch hour, thoroughly enjoying the time you are entitled to.

TIP Leave work behind at the end of the day. Ideally forget about it once you walk out the door. Else use the journey home to switch off. After a difficult day, you may find talking things over with your partner helpful. Allow time for this and then enjoy the rest of your evening.

What activities do you enjoy doing outside work? Try to schedule these activities into your week.

_____

_____

_____

_____

_____

_____

_____

TIP Sleep well. Try to get eight hours of sleep each night. The rest and recovery sleep gives you will help you be your best at work.

TIP Take your annual leave and use it properly. Make it clear to your employer that you are unavailable during this time. Also, resist the temptation to pop into the office or check your email.

Changing jobs

When is it time to move on? Perhaps you have completed the above activities and are still miserable. Maybe you have run out of new challenges or you want to finally pursue your calling. Only you will know. The exercises in the chapter on change may assist you in this process.

TIP If you are considering a career change, talk to people who are already doing the job you are interested in.

Chapter 14

RELATIONSHIP SATISFACTION

This chapter is about getting the most from your relationship with your partner. Research[1] indicates that relationships are good for your happiness and can help reduce stress. Unfortunately, there is a great deal of unhappiness within relationships, else why would the divorce rate be so high? So, although people in relationships may report being happier in more general terms, it is important to consider what is going on within the relationship on a daily basis. Hopefully this chapter will help get the most out of your relationship so you can be one of the happy ones cited in the research.

Relationship satisfaction is about appreciating what you have and getting the best from it. Happiness in a relationship (as in life) does not mean the end of conflict. However, a happy relationship will be able to deal well with conflict so it does not escalate into something so bad it is deemed irreparable. As such, this chapter is divided into two sections: the good and the not so good.

The good

Tell the story of how you and your partner got together. Recall as many details as possible as you relive this moment in your life. Let the good memories come flooding back.

---

[1] Diener, E., Suh, E.M., Lucus, R.E. and Smith, H.L. (1999), Subjective well-being: three decades of progress, *Psychological Bulletin* 125, 276-302.

List the activities you and your partner used to enjoy doing together but have let slip over the years. What ones can you start doing again?

_____

_____

_____

_____

_____

_____

_____

TIP Arrange a date that you know you will both enjoy. Accounting for both of your needs will make both you and your partner feel good.

Write down all the things you love about your partner. Consider their actions, habits, personality as well as their looks.

_____

_____

_____

_____

_____

_____

_____

_____

_____

When your partner shares their good news with you, listen well and be pleased for them. Don't be critical or change the subject. Be there with them during the good times and be proud of their achievements.

List ten reasons why you were glad to have your partner in your life just this last week.

_____

_____

_____

_____

_____

_____

_____

_____

_____

_____

_____

Do small, positive things for your partner. Not because you have to, but because you want to.

Finding time for closeness and intimacy is so important to a relationship. Life gets busy and people get stuck in their routines. Work; children; families – something always seems to get in the way. However, working on ways to be with your partner is time never wasted.

What steps can you take to be more intimate with your partner on a regular basis?

_____

_____

_____

_____

_____

_____

TIP Give your partner lots of hugs. You do not need a reason.

Hold your partner's hand. Whether it's on the sofa, at the movies, or on the street, it doesn't really matter. Such an act can be very comforting and stress relieving. **TIP**

In what ways does your partner show their commitment to you? How do you show your commitment to them?

_____

_____

_____

_____

_____

_____

_____

_____

_____

_____

_____

_____

TIP Write your partner a love letter and post it to them.

Take the time to sit down with your partner and share TIP your hopes and dreams for the future.

What are the things that work in your relationship, which you can rely upon?

_____

_____

_____

_____

_____

_____

_____

_____

TIP Try to focus on the things in your relationship that work, rather than the stuff you know only drives a wedge between the two of you. How will your relationship be a good one if you are only adding bad ingredients to it?

The not so good

Relationship satisfaction does not mean the end of difficulties. However, being able to deal with them in a way that does little harm to your relationship is important to long term happiness. Understanding the basics of conflict resolution may help you work through arguments sooner.

How do you and your partner tend to argue? You will probably find there is a pattern to your actions. Recalling your last argument may help you with this activity.

_____

_____

_____

_____

_____

_____

_____

_____

_____

_____

Conflict resolution is about working together so both you and your partner are happy with the outcome. It is not about giving in, getting aggressive so you get your own way, or avoiding it altogether. Learning to resolve conflict well can make your relationship stronger as you develop mutual respect for one another.

How do you generally resolve your arguments? Do you think you resolve conflict effectively?

_____

_____

_____

_____

_____

_____

_____

_____

The following steps may assist you in working through arguments and resolving them in a healthy manner.

1 DISCUSS THE PROBLEM

Focusing solely on the problem, take it in turns to listen to the other person's needs and concerns. Remember, your partner is entitled to their own opinion and they should be valued and respected. Do not assume you know what the other person is thinking. Nor should you assume they know what you are thinking.

TIP When speaking, use 'I'. For example, "I feel you spend too much time watching television", rather than, "you spend too much time watching television". This way you own the feeling and the statement becomes an opinion, rather than a fact.

TIP If you find yourself reacting particularly strongly to a certain issue, take time to reflect on why it means so much to you. Being able to identify your feelings will enable you to set them aside and hopefully approach the conflict more objectively.

If at any point you realise you have made a mistake **TIP** about something, don't be afraid to acknowledge your error, rather than letting conflict continue.

TIP Look out for the words you use in arguments. Typically the word 'always' will come up. Become aware of what you are doing and replace your words with something more realistic. It will help you put things into perspective.

2 COME UP WITH SOLUTIONS

Now it's time to brainstorm. You need to work together to suggest ways of meeting both sets of needs. Think of as many ideas as possible. Discuss all potential solutions, no matter how impractical they may seem. Do not dismiss any solutions. Respect what the other person says. You should both take a turn.

TIP Remember your partner is not you and as such has differences to you. Learn to value and appreciate them, rather than trying to turn them into a version of you.

3 PROPOSE A SOLUTION

Once you have a good list of solutions, take it in turns to discuss what you think of them. Discard those that you both agree are unacceptable or unrealistic. Try to find solutions that you both feel are suitable. Remember you want a solution that both of you are happy with.

From here you can tweak the proposed solution as necessary until it is something that can be easily implemented.

TIP Remember you cannot change your partner. Only they can change themselves and only you can change you and the role you play within the relationship.

4 IMPLEMENT YOUR AGREED SOLUTION

Finally, you need to decide how the solution is to be carried out. You should both be happy with the outcome. It is no use railroading a person into agreeing with you, since the conflict is bound to come up again and again. Furthermore, that person will be resentful of you and this is not productive to a good relationship. Make sure you are both clear on the exact details.

TIP Keep things in perspective. Don't let one argument about one issue escalate to affect the rest of your relationship. Try to forgive quickly. See the chapter on forgiveness for more on this.

TIP Remember, making time for yourself means you will function better within your relationship. This is where the rest of the book can help. Promote your own happiness.

Given what you have learned about resolving conflict, what will you try to do differently from now on?

_____

_____

_____

_____

_____

_____

Chapter 15

LIVING A LIFE OF PASSION

Thanks to the wonders of the internet and the multitude of reality TV shows, it's all too easy now to sit down and watch other people live their lives. Of course, this is at the expense of you living *your* life. Since it's your life and your life alone, it's worth being an active participant in it. You will be far happier and fulfilled and no longer just a passive observer. The following activities will help ensure you do just that.

It's time to find your passion and get involved in your own life.

Find your passion

For a happier life, one that engages you, you will want to make time for your passion. It is a way of ensuring you are actually living your life, rather than letting life slip away. It also allows you to enjoy the here and now. By making the most of the present means you are less likely to have regrets later on.

Do you know what your passion is? What do you absolutely love and cannot wait to spend time doing? When you are doing it, the hours fly by. You can list more than one thing.

_____

_____

_____

_____

_____

If you already know what your passion is, then good for you. Just make sure you find regular time each week engaged in it. For those of you who are struggling to find something that you truly care about, hopefully the following will help.

List all the things that you used to do, but are no longer doing. Include things from your childhood that you have put on hold for whatever reason and never went back to.

TIP From your list, choose those activities that appeal the most and find time to carry them out. You can always revise a particular activity to fit in with your present lifestyle.

Is there anything you've always wanted to learn or get involved with?

_____

_____

_____

_____

_____

_____

_____

For the items listed above, write down an action plan detailing when and where you are going to begin. How are you going to learn it? How much time each week do you need? Give as many details as possible.

_____

_____

_____

_____

_____

_____

_____

_____

_____

_____

TIP Don't be afraid to try new things. You never know what it will ignite within you.

It is important to follow your dreams, not someone else's. If you worry about what other people think you will never be able to fully commit to what is meaningful and important to you. Do the things you like, not the things you think you should like. Everybody is different and your passion can take its own form.

Flow experience

If you have found your passion, chances are you are experiencing flow on a regular basis. Flow experience is a concept defined by Csikszentmihalyi[1] to describe those moments when you are completely and totally absorbed in an activity. As such, everything else is forgotten. It is about living in the moment and is a great way to boost long term wellbeing and happiness. When you are in a flow experience, your focus is so complete that you forget all about sleeping and eating. You are not even aware of yourself; you are immersed in the activity you are engaged in.

---

[1] You may like to read 'Flow: The Psychology of Optimal Experience' by Mihaly Csikszentmihalyi.

Do you recognise these feelings? Can you recall the last time you had a flow experience?

_____

_____

_____

_____

_____

_____

_____

You can have a flow experience with any activity that is mindful and requires you to actively participate in it. As such, good conversation, reading a novel, playing sport, working on your hobby, letter writing, gardening, even cleaning the house are examples where you can experience flow.

Brainstorm activities you can personally carry out which you think will give a flow experience. You should also include the activities you wanted to try that you listed earlier on, as part of Find Your Passion.

_____

_____

_____

_____

_____

_____

_____

_____

_____

To achieve a flow experience, Csikszentmihalyi outlines three conditions that must be met.

1 Your chosen activity should have a clearly defined set of goals. This will help you focus your energy and give you direction.

Write down the goals of your chosen activity (you can make separate lists for each activity). They can be long term or short term. A later chapter goes into goals in greater detail.

_____

_____

_____

_____

_____

_____

_____

_____

_____

_____

2 There should be a good balance between your perceived skills and perceived challenges. The important point here is that it is about perception. If you believe your skills far surpass the challenge, you will become bored as it will be too easy for you. Whereas if you perceive the challenge as being too hard, you may become frustrated.

Look at your goals. Do you think you have given yourself enough of a challenge with the goals you have set? Will you be learning new things, or will it be fairly routine?

_____

_____

_____

_____

_____

_____

_____

_____

Do you think there may be areas where you will struggle? You need to be honest here.

_____

_____

_____

_____

_____

_____

_____

_____

TIP Modify your goals as needed. You can do this whilst working on your goal, as the challenge changes.

3 Feedback is essential. It will enable you to modify your actions if necessary, to keep you in the flow. The feedback can be negative as well as positive. It can enable you to move on and progress (providing you have the skills to do so).

TIP Schedule time for when you will receive feedback on your progress. Feedback can come in the form of self-reflection, or from other people.

Try to give yourself regular flow experiences. You TIP should give yourself such opportunities on a daily basis.

The next time you experience flow, note down how you feel afterwards.

_____

_____

_____

_____

_____

_____

TIP Avoid multi-tasking. It will help you focus on one task at a time and enable you to do your best at it. Doing two things at once means your attention will be compromised and mistakes can happen. Also, it will stop you from experiencing flow.

Passive activities

Being more active in your life means you'll get the most from it. If this is what you want then you need to be aware of the one major stealer of time – your television. The nature of TV means you are not actively engaged in the activity. You just sit there, watching. As such, you are prevented from doing the things you want to do and of course you will get fewer flow experiences.

How much television do you watch each week? Be honest, nobody's judging! If you are not sure, monitor your habit for a week. How do you feel about this?

Monday:

Tuesday:

Wednesday:

Thursday:

Friday:

Saturday:

Sunday:

Reflections:

How much television would you *like* to be watching each week?

_____

_____

_____

_____

TIP Don't feel compelled to give up television altogether. Watching television offers you a time to relax. It is a chance to escape for a while and forget the troubles of the day. Although it is worth being aware of what you do actually watch. Monitor how you feel afterwards – did it relax you or are you left feeling angry and agitated?

If you want to cut down on television watching, there's no need to go cold turkey. Depending on where you are right now and where you want to be, you can reduce the time gradually until you have reached your goal.

Write your plan here. Note how much television you plan to watch on a daily basis for the first week. Then do the same for the second week, and so on, until you have reached your goal.

_____

_____

_____

_____

_____

_____

_____

How will you spend the time you now have available to you?

_____

_____

_____

_____

_____

_____

TIP

Use television to inspire you into action. Find shows that complement your hobbies and interests.

Once you have started cutting down on your television watching, note how you spent your time here as well as how you felt about it. You can also keep track of your progress in your journal.

_____

_____

_____

_____

_____

_____

_____

_____

_____

Chapter 16

CHANGE

Change is an inevitable part of life. Being able to cope when change happens and being aware of how much change you are personally capable of is an important component for overall happiness. The idea of change is apparent throughout this book – after all if you are promoting happiness in your life then you are bringing about change. However, what this chapter does is to focus on the idea of change, to recognise it is okay and not something to fear. Embracing change will enable you to get the most out of your life.

Knowing what you can change

List the things you think you have control over in your life.

_____

_____

_____

_____

_____

_____

_____

_____

_____

_____

List the things you think are beyond your control.

_____

_____

_____

_____

_____

_____

_____

Recognising how much control you have over your life will directly impact on the amount of change you feel you can bring about. The concept of 'locus of control' is important here (locus of control is a term coined by Julian Rotter[1]). It is about how much you believe control is in your hands, or not.

People with an internal locus of control believe themselves to be in control of their lives and destiny. They will make their own decisions rather than letting other people decide for them. Whereas a person with an external locus of control does not recognise the impact they have over their own life. Instead they see it as being down to luck, fate, or other people's behaviours.

People are generally not either/or as far as this concept is concerned. However, some people may believe in fate more than others and are more willing to let other people make decisions for them.

---

[1] Rotter, J.B. (1966) Generalised expectancies for internal versus external control of reinforcement, _Psychological Monographs_ 80 (609).

To help you identify where your locus of control lies, keep a log of the events in your life and how you explain these events. These events can be large or small depending on the time you have available.

For example: someone praises you at work. How do you explain it? Luck? They must have been in a good mood? You did a good job and it was nice to have been praised for it?

TIP Keep an eye out for faulty thinking. Words such as 'can't', 'must', 'should' and 'always' are an indication that a person is being influenced by external factors.

Keep a record of the decisions you make and times when you let others make decisions for you.

As you progress, do you start to see how much control you have over your daily life? Whether big or small, making your own decisions means you are making changes in your life. Be aware that not making a decision or letting others choose for you is a choice in itself. You have chosen to hand control over to another.

Having an internal locus of control can be very empowering. It enables a person to take control of all aspects of their life – from relationships to work. However, you cannot control and change everything. Although it is easy to underestimate how much control you do have, there are some things you cannot change.

Typical things you cannot change are as follows: being born, who your genetic family are, death, sexuality and choice. Yes, we all have choice. Even not choosing, or allowing another to choose for you is a choice you have made.

However, you still have control over how you choose to respond to the things you cannot control. For instance, you could deny that you are going to die - refusing to accept you are getting older, ever searching for anti-ageing products. Or, you could enjoy getting older, embracing each stage of your life.

Review your list of what you felt you could not control at the start of this chapter. Are they truly valid? Or are they in fact decisions you have made.

_____
_____
_____
_____
_____
_____
_____

Something else you cannot change is other people. You might like them to behave a certain way. Unless they choose to, it just won't happen.

Note the ways you try to change another person or expect them to be like you. Keep an eye out for faulty thinking here.

_____
_____
_____
_____

_____

_____

_____

_____

_____

_____

Reflect on the previous week. What events occurred that were beyond your control? How did you manage?

_____

_____

_____

_____

_____

_____

_____

_____

TIP Own what you say. Use 'I' rather than 'we' or 'you'. Replace 'You start to wonder why you're doing it' with 'I start to wonder why I'm doing it'.

Get excited about change

What changes have you made recently? How did you cope? Are you glad you made them?

_____

_____

_____

_____

_____

_____

_____

_____

_____

List the things you would like to change (large and small) but have yet to get around to.

_____

_____

_____

_____

_____

_____

_____

_____

_____

_____

Spend some time thinking about what factors are preventing change. Write down all your barriers, fears and anxieties. Try to be honest—it is your list and nobody is judging you. This way you can tackle each fear one by one, helping you get a step closer to change.

_____

_____

_____

_____

_____

_____

_____

_____

_____

_____

Look at each barrier logically. What steps can you take to overcome each fear? Do you need to challenge some faulty thinking? Do you need support from others? Use your journal if needed.

_____

_____

_____

_____

_____

_____

_____

_____

_____

_____

Working on your fears in small steps will make them more manageable.

When you make changes or try new things, they become a part of who you are. If you are able to recognise this, then suddenly change does not have to be something to fear. People do adapt, even to great changes. If you take the opportunity to step out of your comfort zone, face your fears and make that change you've always wanted to, you will be glad of it. You are capable of far more than you probably realise.

List five things you would not normally do, but would like to try. Set yourself a deadline and give each one a go. What did you learn from the experience?

_____

_____

_____

_____

_____

_____

_____

_____

_____

_____

_____

_____

TIP Don't hold onto old ways of doing things just because they have always been with you. Think about better, more efficient ways, that you will be happier with. Remember: you make the rules, so feel free to change them.

Detail five small things you have done the same way for many years. How could you do them differently?

_____

_____

_____

_____

_____

_____

_____

_____

TIP If you are uneasy dealing with change, start by making small changes. It can stop you getting into a rut and allows you to be open to trying new things. These small things add up and can help you cope when the larger changes inevitably crop up.

Rather than trying to break a habit you want rid of, **TIP** work to actively replace it with a new one. In the early days you will need to practise your new habit lots, until it is ingrained. However, it should be part of your life within a month.

Let yourself be open to change. Being open-minded and willing to learn will help you on your quest for change.

List all the things you want to learn about in the next year.

_____

_____

_____

_____

_____

_____

_____

_____

_____

_____

_____

_____

If you are struggling to make a change in your life, you may want to look at your values. Is there a conflict between your values and the change you want to make? How will you resolve this? You could change your goal or you could change your values.

The following chapter on goals will help you set up the changes you want to bring about in your life

A word about grief and loss

You are probably not going to come to this book when a loss occurs. However, reading this now will hopefully help you recognise that what you are experiencing is okay.

One of the biggest changes we will all experience is the loss of a loved one, whether it is a person or a pet. What follows is the experience of grief. Grief can affect how you think, feel and behave. It can also affect you physically. It is okay to feel whatever you are feeling. You may experience a wide variety of emotions, including: shock, anger, guilt, denial and depression.

With time, hopefully what follows is resolution and healing, enabling you to move on with your life. There is no set time for working through your grief and it can last for years. It can also last just weeks. There is no right or wrong when it comes to experiencing loss. As time passes, eventually there will come a time when a person will choose: to move on with their life, or stay where they are.

It is important to be aware that people experience grief differently and their responses may be very different to yours. This does not mean they are not grieving. Accept their reactions as normal and it may help prevent any unnecessary upset.

Grief counsellors can help you during any stage of your loss, whether it is days, weeks, months or years after the event. Don't hesitate to seek help if you are struggling to cope.

Who could you turn to for support during a time of loss? Make a list of as many people and resources as possible, so you will have plenty of options.

_____

_____

_____

_____

_____

_____

_____

_____

_____

_____

_____

Chapter 17

GOALS

Having goals in your life can work wonders for your happiness and wellbeing. They give your life a purpose and increase your feelings of hope and optimism. Your goals can be short term or long term. In fact, setting and achieving daily goals will add up to some major accomplishments by the end of the year. And it's all your own work. Of course, by setting yourself regular, meaningful goals you are more likely to experience flow.

You may want to use a pencil for the following activities, since you may need to revise what you have written. Else you could always use your journal to work through this chapter.

Establish your goals

We will begin by writing down your goals. For each type of goal, try to think long term as well as short term. If you like, you can break them down into daily, monthly and yearly goals. Come back as often as you like to add to and revise your lists.

What are your career goals? These can be relevant to your present job as well as future plans you may have.

_____

_____

_____

_____

_____

_____

_____

List your education goals. These may be relevant to now, as well as future plans you may have. It can be both formal and informal forms of education and learning.

_____

_____

_____

_____

_____

_____

_____

What are your financial goals? This could relate to things like money management, saving for something in the immediate future, as well as your long term plans.

_____

_____

_____

_____

_____

_____

_____

_____

_____

_____

What goals do you have with regards your home? This could be the things you want to complete around your house as well as relating to property ownership.

_____

_____

_____

_____

_____

_____

What are your health and fitness goals? Particularly relevant here are exercise and healthy eating. You may also have goals specific to your own health needs.

_____

_____

_____

_____

_____

_____

_____

_____

TIP There is a later chapter on exercise that you can draw upon for additional ideas.

Do you have any relationship goals? Relationships can refer to family, friends, your children, your partner. Think about things you might want to improve upon.

_____

_____

_____

_____

_____

_____

_____

_____

List your leisure goals. How do you want to spend your free time and what do you want to accomplish? Think about hobbies you currently do as well as ones you want to start.

_____

_____

_____

_____

_____

_____

_____

_____

_____

What are your personal development goals?
These are things you want to improve on, learn about or change that don't fall into the above categories

_____

_____

_____

_____

_____

_____

_____

_____

_____

List any other goals you may have.

_____

_____

_____

_____

_____

_____

_____

_____

_____

Review your goals

Having listed your goals, let's do a review, to ensure you have chosen the right goals.

REVIEW: Life balance is important. Do you have a good balance in the goals you have chosen? Are you neglecting certain areas? Revise if necessary.

REVIEW: It is best to only set goals that are truly within your power to meet. As such it is important that they do not rely on the actions of others. Money is another goal to be wary of. Wanting to become a millionaire may work for some, but the reality is, we are not all entrepreneurial types. Aim high yes, but keep it realistic. Review your goals to check they are feasible.

REVIEW: Look at each of your goals. Are they ongoing or do they have an end point? Think carefully about this. For example, lose 5kgs through exercise may seem like an end-point goal. However, what happens then? Make sure you have a plan in place for what you intend to do once your goal is achieved. Can you move on to another goal or will it be something that becomes part of your life? Review each goal as needed, identifying if they are ongoing or have an end point.

REVIEW: Make sure that the goals you have set are for you, not someone else. You should *want* to do them, rather than believing you should do them for whatever reason.

REVIEW: Are your goals challenging enough? To keep your goal interesting you will want a challenge. If it is too easy, you will probably get bored and quickly lose interest. However, if the goal is too challenging, it may be too much for you. You end up feeling disgruntled, uninspired and eventually give up. Revise each of your goals to ensure you have this balance.

Setting up your goals

Having clarified the goals you want to accomplish, you need to establish the details of each of your goals. By doing this you will have all your bases covered and it will make success more likely.

For each of your goals outlined above, write down the details of exactly how you are going to achieve it. List all the steps you need to take and detail when you are going to do each step. This is your action plan. Use a pencil as it will make revisions easier.

You will find your action plan worksheet in the appendix, which you will need to photocopy for each goal. Else you can use your journal.

TIP Don't expect to accomplish your goals overnight. Taking things one small step at a time is a great way to progress.

REVIEW: Review your action plan with an open mind. Ask yourself, is it honestly workable? If you have decided that you are going to do a workout at 6am each morning, but are not a morning person, how likely are you to succeed? Your goals should fit into your lifestyle and match your personality. Make changes as needed.

Can you think of things that could potentially get in the way of you achieving your goals? Think of people as well as life situations that may cause problems for you. For each one of these barriers, write down a plan of action for what you will do if they occur.

Your barriers and solutions worksheet is found in the appendix. Photocopy the sheet for each one of your goals.

Every week or so, review your action plan. Is it still workable? Ideally you want your goals to become part of your regular routine, so keep tweaking until you have accomplished this.

For each of your goals set up a deadline, unless it is an ongoing goal. Remember dates can always be moved if necessary (after all, you set the date so you can change it). Allow yourself extra time and use your action plan as a guide.

Goal	Deadline

Achieving your goals

You have your goals and a plan of action. The important thing now is that you go on and achieve your goals.

For bigger goals you may want to reward the steps you have made as you progress. Such rewards can be anything you like so long as they do not undermine your goal in any way. To be really effective, make them something that you cannot get any other way.

Activity: Which goals should you reward? Write these down. Now list your rewards and when you will receive them.

Goal	Reward	When receive

TIP If you reward yourself when you haven't really earned it, you are only letting yourself down.

List those qualities, characteristics, skills, experiences and talents that you can draw upon to help you achieve your goals.

_____

_____

_____

_____

_____

_____

What positive steps have you taken in the past when faced with unexpected hurdles? Which ones benefited you most? Select those you could draw upon if needed.

_____

_____

_____

_____

_____

_____

Learn to argue with the part of yourself that says to just give up. Tell that self 'no! I am going to keep going'. Really mean it. I mean, REALLY mean it. **TIP**

TIP Keep an eye out for faulty thinking. It may be getting in the way of you achieving your goals, so take the time to work through your thoughts.

Note down the support you can draw upon to help you achieve each of your goals.

_____

_____

_____

_____

_____

_____

TIP For longer goals, every month or so remind yourself of why you wanted to achieve that goal in the first place.

List your distractions. That is, the things you do that are getting in the way of your progress. These are the things you typically do as well as ones relevant to a particular goal.

_____

_____

_____

_____

_____

_____

TIP Set up a time when you will allow yourself to focus on your distractions. This way you know you can indulge in these things, knowing you have made good progress on your goals.

Don't underestimate the power of imagery. Close your eyes and relax. Now imagine you are working on your goal. Invoke positive feelings towards it and how good it feels being immersed in the activity. Spend time getting into the mood. Now imagine you have achieved your goal. How does it feel? Imagery can assist when you are starting to falter.

TIP If you like, put notes or pictures around your house that remind you of your goal. Review them on a regular basis. As you get used to them being there, they lose their impact, so move them around or make new ones.

TIP When working on your goals, remember to enjoy the journey along the way.

Chapter 18

GRATITUDE

Gratitude is about having an awareness of and appreciation for the good things in your life and not taking them for granted. Practising gratitude has consistently been shown to be beneficial to overall happiness[1]. It may increase life satisfaction, enhance social support and help prevent stress and depression. You may even sleep better. It is a very positive emotion; after all it is hardly likely that a person can feel bitter, angry and resentful at the same time as feeling grateful.

Reflect on how grateful you think you are right now. Is it something you give much thought to, or until this moment not given it a consideration? Be honest with yourself here.

_____

_____

_____

_____

_____

When you are grateful, you are focusing on what you have got rather than obsessing about what you have not got. It means you are valuing the people in your life and the possessions you do have, as well as your own skills, abilities and the role you play to make the world a better place.

---

[1] For example: McCullough, M. E.,Tsang, J., & Emmons, R.A. (2004) Gratitude in intermediate affective terrain: Links of grateful moods with individual differences and daily emotional experience, *Journal of Personality and Social Psychology, 86*, 295–309.

How might being more grateful benefit you personally?

_____

_____

_____

_____

_____

_____

By practising gratitude now, it can help you through the most difficult of times as you recognise that your life is not all bleak. Focusing your attention on the good things and people in your life helps you perceive the world differently. Nothing has changed, just your attitude. There are a number of ways to go about this and they are not difficult to do.

List five good things about your life, as it is right now.

_____

_____

_____

_____

_____

_____

_____

_____

Keeping a gratitude journal is consistently shown in studies to increase happiness[1].

Set aside space in your journal to record things you are grateful for. Spend a few minutes each day reflecting and writing about the good things in your life. Try to notice things you would normally take for granted. Do this in addition to the activities that follow.

TIP Say thank you on a regular basis.

Consider all the different areas of your life. List the things you are grateful for in that area. For example with work, perhaps you are grateful you only have a 20 minute commute to work. You can expand on this activity in your journal.

_____

_____

_____

_____

_____

_____

_____

_____

_____

_____

_____

[1] For example: Emmons, R.A., & McCullough, M.E. (2003) Counting blessings versus burdens: Experimental studies of gratitude and subjective well-being, _Journal of Personality and Social Psychology, 84_, 377-389.

Keep an eye out for faulty thinking that is getting in the way of you feeling gratitude. Challenge thoughts such as 'nothing good ever happens to me', 'my life is the worst', 'bad things always come my way'.

Write a letter of gratitude to someone who has made a positive impact on your life. If you can, send it to them. Even better, read it to them.

Take the time every now and then to step back and appreciate what you have. Such regular reflection can help prevent you taking your life for granted.

Recall a negative event in your life and how you got through it. Think about how other people helped you during this time.

_____

_____

_____

_____

_____

_____

_____

Look for other people's good deeds and know that the world is better for that act.

When doing catch-up emails to friends and family reflect on the good things in your life as well as the people who supported you through a trying time and let this be the focus of your email.

At the end of each week that you have practised gratitude, monitor how you are feeling. Do you notice any positive changes? Has it improved how you think about your life and go about your day?

_____

_____

_____

_____

_____

_____

_____

_____

TIP The grass may be greener on the other side – and if you search hard enough you will probably find it. However, if you really want a happy life, work at being grateful for the unique colour of your own grass.

Chapter 19

KINDNESS AND GENEROSITY

It's an interesting fact that giving to others makes us feel better about ourselves. Taking the time to be kind and thoughtful enhances happiness and wellbeing and gives us a greater sense of purpose. When you start being kinder, you will begin to recognise how much you have to offer, no matter who you are. During these times, you will find you have forgotten yourself and your own concerns. Your worries go on hold, as you stop focusing inwardly.

Such acts of altruism could be regarded as selfish, yet if everybody benefits what's the problem? Is it better to give your time at the local shelter, helping others in a positive way, as well as boosting your mood, or to stay home watching TV, sneering at the do-gooders out there making a difference?

You may like to keep a note in your journal of the impact the following activities and tips have on your life. Was there anything that surprised you? Note the changes in yourself, including your willingness to go out of your way to help others.

Reflect back on last week. Recall times when you were giving to others – whether it was your time or your money.

Did you struggle with the above task? Is it something you would like to change?

_____

_____

_____

_____

_____

Currently, how do you feel when you give to others? Can you see the benefits or do you see it as a burden? Be honest.

_____

_____

_____

_____

_____

How much do you gossip or say bad things about others? Keep an eye on yourself and record your findings here. Were you surprised by your behaviour?

_____

_____

_____

_____

_____

_____

_____

Brainstorm ways you can be kinder in your everyday life. What specific skills, attributes, knowledge and resources do you have that may aid another? Use this list to help you get started in your quest to be kinder. The tips that follow may assist you with this activity.

_____

_____

_____

_____

_____

_____

_____

TIP You don't always need to go for the grand gesture when being kind. Any act, not matter how small makes a difference. Look for these opportunities in your life. It will change how you see the world.

Look for opportunities to say something nice about another person, whether it is to their face or when they are not around. **TIP**

TIP Compliment someone. Make sure you mean it though. Don't say something just for the sake of it.

Give someone a small gift, to let them know you are thinking of them. **TIP**

TIP

Come to the aid of a stranger. Don't be the one to keep walking, assuming another will assist.

Phone a friend and find out how they're doing. Resist TIP the temptation to use it as an excuse to talk about yourself. Really listen and empathise.

If you wonder why you should bother being kinder, reflect on how it feels when someone is kind to you.

_____

_____

_____

_____

_____

Write down the good things you do for another person in the week ahead. It can be a kind act as well as a kind word. If you like, you can continue this activity on a weekly basis, noting your findings in your journal.

_____

_____

_____

_____

_____

A powerful act is to carry out a deed anonymously. That is, you do something good for another person, without them knowing it was you. Note what you did and how you felt about it.

_____

_____

_____

_____

_____

_____

_____

What charities or organisations do you support? What could you do to get more involved?

_____

_____

_____

_____

_____

_____

_____

TIP Remember charity shops? If you don't already, give your unwanted possessions to charity, rather than selling them. What were you going to do with the money anyway? Was it going to change your life for the better in the long term?

Research consistently shows that volunteering increases happiness and the more you do the happier you are[1].

Do you volunteer? Have you noticed the benefits it brings? If you are not volunteering right now, note times in the past when you have helped others, for no financial payment.

_____

_____

_____

_____

_____

TIP Do volunteer work on a regular basis. You could work with a group of people you have never encountered before or know very little about. For an even bigger challenge you could take this as an opportunity to confront your prejudices and work with a group you fear or dislike.

Name your prejudices. Confronting and admitting your prejudices may not be easy. Try to be honest with yourself here. Maybe ask yourself if you ever make 'all or nothing', or 'always' statements about particular groups of people.

_____

_____

_____

_____

_____

[1] For example: Thoits, P. A. & L. N. Hewitt (2001) Volunteer Work and Well-Being, _Journal of Health and Social Behavior_, 42(2). 115-31.

TIP Try to see the good in everyone. Everyone has redeeming qualities and assets.

Keep an eye on someone you dislike. For a week notice their good qualities and the good things they do. You may not find this easy as it will make it harder for you to dislike them. Note your findings – about the other person as well as about yourself.

_____

_____

_____

_____

_____

_____

_____

TIP Don't expect each act to be appreciated. This is not why you are doing it. You are doing them because you want to, not for the thanks. You are better off assuming your efforts won't be acknowledged. This will help ensure you won't feel resentment if people don't respond as you'd imagined. This resentment can lead you to deciding that it is pointless being kind as it gets you nowhere.

If you want to know how to be kinder to yourself, proceed to the next chapter.

Chapter 20

STRESS, STRESS MANAGEMENT & RELAXATION

Understanding and managing your stress is an important skill to have if you want a happier life. I hope you recognise now that this book is not a magic wand that will somehow rid you of all misery forever. Happy people are not immune to the stressful events that occur in life. However, this chapter hopes to assist you in managing your stress when it arises, to understand the importance of relaxation and discover what personally works for you. The outcome being that you are not overwhelmed by stress; rather you bounce back sooner and are ultimately happier for longer.

What is stress?

Stress is a personal response to life events. It can be brought about in many ways: through the actions, thoughts and emotions of ourselves, by other people as well as our environment. The things that cause stress are known as stressors. These stressors can be major life changes (e.g. moving house), or smaller events (deadline at work). However, if we do not deal with the small things, they can build up and our stress can become out of control.

TIP Not all stress is bad. Positive stressors can enhance our ability to perform well and push us into achieving that all-important goal. However, prolonged or severe stress not dealt with properly can be harmful to us both physically and mentally and can lead to burnout.

Identify your stressors

Are you aware of the events in your life that bring on stress? You may want to monitor your life for a week and note the stressors that are causing you upset or getting you down. Consider the following areas: your home, work, education, leisure, general routine (including time management) as well as your relationships with others. Use your journal if needed.

_____

_____

_____

_____

_____

_____

_____

_____

_____

Of your stressors listed above, which areas would you most like to change? You might like to rank them in order of importance.

_____

_____

_____

_____

_____

_____

_____

_____

_____

The stress response

When we experience stress our body goes through a number of changes. These include: an increase in heart rate and blood pressure, a rise in blood sugar levels and adrenaline is produced through the adrenal glands causing stimulation of the heart and organs. This is known as a stress response.

Effective stress relief aims to ease this response, since if these changes are experienced regularly, health risks may arise and can include the following:

- Coronary heart disease
- Neuroses
- Diabetes mellitus
- Ulcers
- Asthma
- Migraine
- Psychoses

Your stress symptoms

How do you know you are experiencing stress? Having identified areas of your life that contribute to your stress, it is also important that you are able to identify your symptoms. In other words, what is the outcome you experience as a result of the stressors in your life?

The symptoms of stress are many and varied, but typical symptoms are as follows:

Behavioural	Physical
Lethargic	Headaches
Drinking more	Shaking
Eating more/less	Stomach problems
Smoking more	High blood pressure
Sleep problems	Nausea
Sexual problems	Dizziness
	Increased sweating
Psychological	**Emotional**
Procrastination	Mood swings
Lack of concentration	Frequent crying
Negative thoughts	Irritable
Blaming self	Anxious
Feeling confused	Feeling depressed

Are you aware of experiencing any of these symptoms? You may want to keep note of your symptoms in the week ahead. Consider your behaviour, thoughts, physical and emotional changes. Write down when you experienced the particular symptom.

_____
_____
_____
_____
_____
_____
_____
_____

Managing your stress

What steps do you currently take to relieve stress?

_____

_____

_____

_____

_____

_____

How effective do you find such strategies?

_____

_____

_____

_____

_____

TIP Are you aware of the things people often do to try and relieve stress which are not actually effective? Alcohol, smoking and eating sugary and fatty foods (the ones you turn to at times of stress) can also trigger the stress response. When we manage stress effectively we bring about physical changes that reduce the associated health risks that arise from ongoing stress. It is important therefore that you do the right thing, rather than what is commonly assumed will help.

It may not surprise you to learn that it is your personal response to the stressful events in your life that impacts on the subsequent symptoms you experience.

Here is an example:

Stressor: working long hours.

Stress symptoms: headaches, tired, irritable and confused.

This appears to make sense by itself. You're working long hours and end up with headaches. However, the missing component is your personal response to working long hours. You may say to yourself that you must work hard or you will be fired, and are therefore putting extra pressure on yourself through your thinking. If on the other hand, you see working long hours as an opportunity to make more money, relish the challenge and enjoy the experience, chances are you would not experience the stress symptoms.

How you think has a big impact on your life and can impact on how you handle stressors. This in turn will impact on your emotions, behaviours and physical symptoms.

TIP It makes sense to review Part Two which introduced you to faulty thinking. Using the described techniques is an important way of managing your stress. They will aid your feelings of control and stop you feeling overwhelmed. Remember challenging faulty thinking is relevant to many situations in your life.

What follows are other skills and activities you can use to add to your stress management plan.

Another valuable skill you can learn to help you deal with your inappropriate thinking is self-talk. What you say to yourself has a huge impact on what you believe, how you feel and consequently how you behave. Thinking negatively may well increase your levels of stress. By swapping this negative self-talk for more positive, constructive words may help you see the situation differently and you may no longer respond with stress.

It is likely that you have discovered your own negative self-talk when working on your faulty thinking. It is also likely you have disputed such beliefs. However, what this task does is allows you to replace the negative thought for a positive one.

Over the next week, keep a note of the negative things you say to yourself. In particular, keep an eye out for negative things you say *about* yourself. Now, you need to replace this statement with a more realistic, positive statement, making sure it is believable.

Event	Negative self-talk	Positive statement
Taking an exam	I will fail	I have prepared well for the exam and know what to expect. I may not get top marks but at least I will have done my best.

THOUGHT STOPPING

Thought stopping can be used in conjunction with positive self-talk to help you take control of your thoughts. This technique will take some practise and it is best if you do it at home to begin with.

Work thought the following steps:

1. Bring to mind an unproductive thought. It may be useful to think of one that occurs fairly frequently.
2. As the thought comes to mind, shout out 'stop' or clap your hands together and imagine a giant stop sign in your head. This will interrupt the intruding thought.
3. Then replace the thought with a more realistic thought. In other words, challenge your thinking.

This technique takes practise but persevere. You will need to do it until you no longer need to shout 'stop' or clap your hands – imagining the stop sign will be enough. Although the technique requires you to deliberately think of an unproductive thought, you can use this technique each time an unrealistic thought automatically comes into your head when you are facing your stressors.

It is well worth knowing how to relax your body and mind. When you are in a relaxed state, tension levels are reduced and the symptoms associated with stress are reversed. Be aware that your body cannot feel stressed and relaxed at the same time. Not only will you be better able to cope with existing stressors, but you are more able to cope with future stressful events.

TIP Practise progressive muscle relaxation. It may take a while to master, but once achieved, you'll wonder how you ever coped without it. You might like to use your journal to record how you feel before and after and the changes that occur over time. Try doing it on a daily basis.

Here is a step-by-step approach to progressive muscle relaxation:

1) Find a warm, comfortable room, free from interruption. Wear loose comfortable clothing. If you have any relaxation music, feel free to use it, although it is not necessary.

2) Lie on your back or sit down in a comfortable position.

3) Rest your arms at your sides, palms facing down.

4) Inhale and exhale slowly and deeply.

5) As you breathe, clench your hands into fists and squeeze them for 15 seconds. Focus on your fists only, feeling the tension in the muscles.

6) Then let your hands relax. Feel the release of tension from the muscles.

7) Continue in this way working through your body.

8) You will want to tense and relax your face, shoulders, back, stomach, pelvis, legs, feet, and toes.

9) Hold for 15 seconds and then relax your body for 30 seconds before moving on. As you relax, your body will feel like it is sinking into the ground.

10) By the end your body will feel really heavy and relaxed. Lie still for a moment, enjoying this state of being.

11) Open your eyes, sit up, then get on with your day.

OTHER STRESS MANAGEMENT TIPS

Below you will find a list of things you can do to help you manage your stress long term. Go through the list and make a note of those things you are already doing in your life. Make a note of when you do them and how often. It is important to do them on a regular basis to obtain maximum benefits.

Then, make a note of those items that you are not already doing, but would like to try. You will need to decide when you will do them and how often. If you do something frequently enough it will soon become part of your life.

Exercise. People who exercise regularly suffer less from stress and have less stress related illness than those who do not exercise regularly[1]. A later chapter focuses on exercise.

_____

_____

_____

_____

-----

[1] There is lots of research support for this. See this paper: Gosselin, C. & Taylor, A. (1999) Exercise as a stress management tool, *Stress News*, Vol 11 No 4.

Make sure your **life is balanced** and is not all about work. Make time for friends, family, yourself, social events and hobbies.

Attend a **yoga** class, or buy a DVD, which you can use at home.

Try **tai chi**.

Deep breathing. This is particularly helpful when faced with a potentially stressful situation. Breathe slowly in through your nose and out through your mouth, filling up your lungs as you do so.

Laugh! Look at the next chapter for more on this.

Relaxation tapes.

Talk to someone – whether it is a friend, family member or counsellor. Read the chapter on support (chapter 11) for more on this.

Have a sense of humour – it can help distance you from the stressor and can give perspective on the situation.

Get yourself a pet. A study in America[1] had stockbrokers look after a pet. When they later encountered a situation that would normally cause stress, these stockbrokers' blood pressure levels were half that of those who did not get to look after a pet.

Have a massage.

Have a bath. Use your favourite oils and for maximum relaxation light some candles.

---

[1] Allen, K. (2003) Are pets a healthy pleasure? The influence of pets on blood pressure, *Current Directions in Psychological Science*, 12, 236-239.

Read a book.

Indulge in your favourite hobby. You could always try something new, that you know you will enjoy.

Eat a healthy diet.

Limit your intake of alcohol and caffeine.

Don't smoke.

Take your annual leave. Give yourself regular breaks and try to slot a regular vacation into your schedule.

Sleep well.

_____

_____

_____

Write down your assets and strengths and place it where
you can refer to it when you need inspiration.

_____

_____

_____

_____

Schedule time to relax. Based on the above, write
down your plans here, to help act as an incentive for
action.

_____

_____

_____

_____

_____

_____

_____

_____

TIP Remember to speak to your doctor if you are
particularly worried about any symptoms you are
experiencing.

Chapter 21

LAUGHTER

A whole chapter dedicated to laughter? This is because laughter is a quick and easy way to promote happiness.

How do you feel about laughter? Do you think there is a time and place for laughing or are you the sort of person who looks for any opportunity for a good laugh?

_____

_____

_____

_____

_____

_____

The act of laughing brings physiological and psychological benefits. When we laugh the part of the brain known as the nucleus accumbens is triggered, which in turn releases the chemical dopamine. When dopamine is released, mood is increased. Laughter also releases muscle tension, which helps you relax. Other benefits include a boost to the immune system as well as lowering of blood pressure. Laughter may also release endorphins which help relieve pain.

TIP Laugh at yourself. This may not be easy, but life doesn't seem nearly as bad when you are able to do this. When you mess up or say something silly, let your defences down for a moment and just have a good chuckle.

Being able to laugh at life, yourself and your situation, puts you in a better position for coping. It can act as a buffer against the reality that life isn't always great. As such it may aid recovery from depression. Seeing the lighter side of life really helps put things into perspective. Life cannot be all bad if there is still something to laugh about. It can help a person rise to a challenge, rather than be defeated by it. Not surprising then, it is an indication of good self-esteem.

When did you last have a good belly laugh? Give the details of when and where and who you were with.

_____

_____

_____

_____

_____

_____

Laughter is also a social experience. Although you can sit and watch a funny film on your own, it is always a pleasure to laugh with friends and share jokes and funny stories. The great thing about laughter is that it is contagious. You laugh, others laugh. It can bring people together, release tensions and reduce conflict.

Who are the people in your life that make you laugh? Who can you share funny stories with?

_____

_____

_____

_____

_____
_____
_____

TIP Make someone laugh. You don't have to tell a joke if that's not your thing. Instead think of humorous ways to cheer up a friend or family member, such as sharing amusing memories. Look for opportunities to make a child giggle.

Promoting laughter

Use your journal to record how laughter makes a difference to your day, week, month and ultimately, life.

The following activities and tips will help highlight different sources of laughter. Try to schedule time to indulge in some laughter therapy.

Humour is a personal thing. As such, you can be the one who decides what comedies are funny and which comedians make you laugh. Don't waste your time watching something that only irritates you, believing you should find it funny. **TIP**

Who are your favourite comedians?

_____
_____
_____
_____

Schedule time to go see a live comedy performance.

List websites that make you laugh. If you don't have any, spend time doing some research so you can build up a list. Maybe ask friends with a similar humour to yours what their favourites are.

_____

_____

_____

_____

_____

Which books make you laugh? You may want to seek out authors that use humour in their writing as well as any comic books that take your fancy.

_____

_____

_____

_____

_____

TIP If you find driving stressful, find funny audio books or podcasts that you can listen to whilst driving.

List your favourite comedy shows and funny movies.

TIP The next time you are at home ill, stick a comedy on. It'll help pass the time, raise your spirits and you may get better sooner.

When you have a bad start to the day, don't let it ruin the rest of your day. Instead, look for the funny side and have a laugh about it with others. TIP

TIP As you go about your day, keep a look out for funny things to make you and other people laugh. It can change how you perceive the world.

There are of course times when laughter is inappropriate. For example, laughing at another person's misfortunes. Instead, imagine you are in their shoes, recognise how they are feeling, then reach out and help them. When you go to laugh at another person, ask yourself how you would feel if another person were to laugh at you for exactly the same reason. Be honest now. If you don't think you'd like it, don't do it.

TIP Laugh *with* others rather than *at* others. It is important to make this distinction. Making a fool of another in order to get a laugh is not the way forward.

Chapter 22

EXERCISE

Exercise is a great way to promote a happier life. Not only does it relieve symptoms of stress and anxiety, it also boosts mood and may even help prevent depression. Furthermore, engaging in exercise is a great way to achieve a flow experience, which as you know provides opportunities for feeling great about yourself. You are doing something that requires focus and attention. Goals and challenges can be set and achieved. Your body image may improve when you exercise regularly. Even without obvious changes to your shape or size, exercising can help you have a more positive perception of self.

Exercise also brings physical as well as mental health benefits[1]. It protects against injury, strengthens bones (which can help prevent osteoporosis) and lowers blood pressure. It can help prevent the onset of Type 2 diabetes. Exercise can also help you lose weight and then maintain a healthy weight. It can reduce the risk of stroke, cardiovascular disease and the development of some cancers. You may even sleep better.

TIP These are just some of the many benefits of exercise. Spend some time learning about the multitude ways exercise can benefit you. Some reasons may matter to you more than others, so keep these in mind as you launch into your exercise programme.

Overall, exercise is a simple, effective means of looking after yourself. It should be done on a regular basis and become part of your life. The rest of this chapter will help you set up an exercise habit and help keep you motivated. If all goes well,

---

[1] See Harvard Medical School Special Health Report, 2007: *Exercise: a Program You Can Live With.*

you will soon come to notice the times when you don't exercise rather than when you do.

TIP Forget about expecting to see great changes in just a few weeks. Changes to your body take time. Expecting immediate results means you are more likely to give up when those changes don't happen.

If you are not as active as you once were, think back to times when you were more active. Reflect on what you did and how you felt.

_____

_____

_____

_____

_____

Speak to a doctor if you have not exercised in a long time, or have any related concerns that may affect your ability to exercise.

How much and what type?

Over the years, recommendations have changed about how much exercise we should do each week – ranging from 30 minutes of moderate activity five days a week, to an hour a day. The important thing I think is to just get started and do what works for you. If you currently do no exercise at all, then 10 minutes a day 3 times a week is a positive step forward. It allows you to establish a routine and work within your capability.

Speak to people you know who exercise on a regular basis. Ask them why they enjoy it. Let them inspire you into action.

For overall fitness and a balanced programme you want to include cardiovascular workouts as well as those that include strength and flexibility.

Cardiovascular exercise is aerobic activity that gets the heart rate up and uses all the major muscle groups. Types of cardio exercise include: football, rugby, hockey, volleyball, netball, squash, badminton, tennis, dancing, running, walking and swimming.

List aerobic activities that you currently enjoy or are interested in trying.

_____

_____

_____

_____

_____

_____

_____

_____

Strength training is important for increasing muscle and bone strength. Ideally is should be carried out 2-3 times a week. Strength is accomplished through working with weights or your own resistance. Visiting the gym or finding a strength workout DVD are two easy ways of building strength. Some types of yoga also build strength.

What strength training do you currently do? If this is something you do not currently do, how might you begin a strength programme?

_____

_____

_____

_____

The final component of a good exercise programme is flexibility. Increasing flexibility is good for the muscles and joints and can help prevent injury. Pilates and yoga give particular focus to flexibility. However, incorporating stretching into your cardiovascular and strength training will also be beneficial.

How much flexibility work do you currently do? What activities are you interested in trying to increase your flexibility?

_____

_____

_____

_____

TIP Set goals for each type of exercise. For example: cardio: run 4km; strength: do a full push up; flexibility: touching your toes without bending your knees.

Getting ready to exercise

Exercise should be something you enjoy and suits your personality. Taking the time to set up a programme that feels right for you increases your chance of success.

TIP Read the chapter on goals to help you refine the details of your exercise programme. It will enable you to work through potential barriers and schedule times that are appropriate to you. There is a section on setting up fitness related goals.

TIP You may also want to consider the chapter on change (especially the section on getting excited about change), if you are struggling to make the first step.

Don't run before you can walk. Expecting to be ready **TIP** for a marathon when you haven't exercised in years will only lead to disappointment. Remember exercise should be a part of your everyday life. As such you can take your time and watch your gradual progress. You are doing it for you and nobody else.

Where do you want to do your workout? Do you prefer being indoors, outdoors, at a gym or at home?

_____

_____

_____

_____

Who do you want to work out with? Do you want to exercise alone, side by side with others, or as part of a team?

_____

_____

_____

_____

_____

_____

What types of activity interest you? Remember to consider the three components of exercise: cardiovascular, strength and flexibility.

_____

_____

_____

_____

_____

_____

What do you need to begin your programme? List everything needed. Consider things like applying for gym membership, purchasing workout DVDs, fitness wear and any equipment needed.

_____

_____

_____

_____

_____

_____

Schedule a time to purchase everything you need. If you find yourself procrastinating, maybe what you are planning isn't right for you. Be honest and revise your plans if need be.

There is a multitude of workout DVDs available, aimed **TIP** at different levels of fitness. Do your research before making a purchase. Some websites offer specific guides to workout DVDs so you can choose one that feels right for you.

List your workout schedule here. Detail what you are going to do, the days and times and for how long. You may prefer to write it up on a separate sheet of paper which you can put up somewhere convenient.

_____

_____

_____

_____

_____

_____

_____

_____

_____

_____

_____

TIP Write your schedule on a calendar.

Don't plan your exercise session when you know you may have to cancel it.

Remember to warm up before you exercise and cool down and stretch after you have exercised.

Keeping motivated

The following tips can be used to keep you motivated, both in the early days and as you continue on your journey.

Challenge your thinking if necessary. You may find your thoughts getting in the way of you actually starting an exercise programme, as well as during the early days where you expect unrealistic improvements.

It is okay to expect to work hard at any exercise. However, don't let it be beyond your capability. You may struggle to keep up, get fed up and give up. Try to get a good balance between your skills and the challenge.

If you don't like what you are doing, declaring it too hard, too easy or too boring, know that it is within your power to change it.

Recognise that you cannot fail. If you miss a session, don't give up. Simply start again tomorrow.

TIP Be proud of all your successes and share them with others who you know will also be proud of you.

Keep it varied. As your muscles get used to an exercise **TIP** they are no longer working as hard. Mixing things up surprises both your body and mind.

TIP Read health and fitness magazines and websites to inspire you and learn from. Increasing your knowledge and expertise helps make it a part of your life.

Other people can be a great source of support to get **TIP** you and keep you in the exercise mindset. Try involving a friend or family member. Perhaps you might consider using a personal trainer.

TIP To help your motivation in the early days, you could reward yourself each time you exercise. You could also reward yourself when you reach certain goals. Just make sure the reward does not undermine the hard work you have done.

Keep a record of the work you are doing. You can track your progress as well as improvements you are seeing in both your fitness and life in general.

TIP If you think you are too tired to exercise, just give it a go. Exercise gives you an energy boost. Tell yourself you'll just go for 10 minutes. Chances are, once you start you'll keep going for longer.

Use a pedometer to track the steps you take throughout the day. Exercise is a simple way of getting a great number of steps in. Aim for 10,000 steps a day. You could set this is one of your goals.

Your exercise sessions may not feel easy. In fact, if it does you are probably not working hard enough. Be okay with this and start to recognise just how powerful and incredible your body is. Don't be afraid to push yourself. Just make sure to stop if you feel pain.

Now remember:

Exercise is all part of you promoting a happier life. So it should not make you miserable. You may need to persist to find something you enjoy. You may also need to persist at an activity to see its benefits. Enjoy the challenge.

Chapter 23

SUNSHINE

One quick way to promote your mood and overall happiness is by stepping outside into the sunshine.

When you go outside, vitamin D is produced when you are exposed to ultraviolet B rays. Vitamin D helps produce serotonin, a hormone that boosts mood. You will also have more energy and it will help you sleep better. An association has been found between vitamin D levels and mental ability, with people who had low levels of the vitamin performing worse on tasks of mental agility. A vitamin D deficiency has also been associated with depression. There are few dietary sources of vitamin D.

TIP You can take a vitamin D supplement; however you should speak to a doctor first, as taking too much may cause health problems.

It takes just a few minutes of exposure to the sun each day to get your vitamin D needs met. However, people with dark skins will need to be exposed to the sun for longer, because the skin pigmentation offers natural protection from the sun. Since it is ultraviolet B rays that lead to the production of vitamin D, you will need to get outside without sun protection, because sunscreen blocks ultraviolet B rays.

TIP Sunshine, like most things in life should be enjoyed in moderation. Too much exposure and you put yourself at risk of skin cancer. However, five minutes a day is good for you.

When outside take a moment to appreciate your TIP surroundings. Wonder at its beauty. Even if you are surrounded by buildings, get curious about the people inside them and the lives they lead as well as admiring the workmanship of the buildings themselves.

What steps can you take to make sure you get your daily sunshine quota?

_____

_____

_____

_____

_____

TIP If you cannot get outdoors, try sitting near a window. There is some research[1] that suggests people who sat by a window reduced their stress sooner than those that did not. A sunny room is not enough to get exposure to ultraviolet B rays, but it may help you feel better.

[1] Kahn Jr., P.H., Friedman, B., Gill, B., Hagman, J., Severson, R.L., Freier, N.G., Feldman, E.N., Carrere, S., Stolyer, A. (2008) A plasma display window?—The shifting baseline problem in a technologically mediated natural world, _Journal of Environmental Psychology_,Vol 28, 2, pp192-199.

Chapter 24

FOOD

What you eat can have a great impact on your mood and energy levels. This chapter details some of those foods known for their uplifting properties. Note such foods are good for both body and mind. Following this, you will consider your relationship with food and ideas to help you deal with emotional eating.

· **Take a look at the following mood boosting foods:**

Nuts
Wholegrains
Tofu
Garlic*
Capsicum*
Chickpeas
Pumpkin seeds
Cheese
Beans
Baked potatoes
Bananas
Eggs
Spinach*
Oats
Blueberries*

These foods all contain zinc, magnesium and the essential amino acid tryptophan. Tryptophan raises your serotonin levels. Serotonin helps boost mood and increase feelings of resilience. You will also feel more comfortable and relaxed.

You can develop feelings of anxiety and depression if you are deficient in these nutrients.

* These foods are also good sources of vitamin C.

Vitamin C helps protect your immune system during times of stress. It is found in many fruits and vegetables, in particular:

Broccoli
Blackcurrants
Brussels sprouts
Kiwi fruit
Watercress
Any citrus fruit
Melon

TIP Try to put as many of these foods onto your shopping list as possible each week.

Foods and drinks to avoid

- Foods containing high sugar

Sugary foods generally have little nutritional content. They give you a quick energy boost that doesn't last, leaving you feeling lethargic soon after. Such foods do little to increase mood and are more likely to leave you feeling stressed.

- Alcohol

Alcohol is a depressant, which will make you feel worse not better.

- Too much caffeine

Caffeine can over stimulate, therefore doing little to calm you or relieve stress. It is more likely to exacerbate symptoms of stress. Too much may also prevent you from sleeping.

TIP For health reasons, it's also a good idea to cut down on foods high in saturated fat, trans fat and salt.

Your relationship with food

We all need food to live. This is a given. Food can also be a great source of pleasure. It is a chance to engage our senses in something delicious. It also offers social opportunities – going out for dinner with friends or chatting with family at the dinner table after a day apart.

However, sometimes food can get in the way of happiness. When you are feeling sad, stressed, worried, powerless and angry suddenly food seems the only solution. Rather than eating when you are hungry, you let your emotions determine when to eat (as well as what, quite often). You have ended up with a relationship with your food that is far more complex than it should be.

Take the time to reflect on your relationship with food. Think about how it may have changed over time. How do you use food? Do you enjoy food? You may like to use your journal to explore this issue further.

_____

_____

_____

_____

_____

_____

_____

_____

_____

Be aware that when you turn to food during difficult times, although it may seem a comfort, you have not changed anything (except maybe your health and waistline). Your problems aren't solved, your stress isn't gone. It may however bring on a new emotion: guilt. This in turn is enough to turn to good old food once more in the hopes it will bring comfort.

For one week keep a record of what you eat and when you eat it. Tune into when you use your emotions to determine when and what you eat. Is it certain emotions that draw you to food? Notice if there are changes in what you eat when you are in a particular mood. Try to be aware also of how much you are eating.

What you need is to learn how NOT to use food for coping with everything else that is going on with your life. The ideal situation is to enjoy your food for what it is and nothing more. Something tasty and nutritious that provides your body with the energy you need to survive.

Throughout this workbook I have given you many tips, insights and ideas into ways to make your life a happier one. Following these ideas will also help prevent you from turning to food to deal with life. Consider the following:

TIP Keep an eye out for faulty thinking. This can occur before you turn to food as a solution (everybody hates me) and also after you have eaten for comfort (I am a failure for eating that bar of chocolate).When you do have days when you feel food is the only way to go, forgive yourself when it happens. It is not the end of the world and you have not failed. I talked about faulty thinking in Part Two and have mentioned it throughout.

Write down what things give you pleasure and help you relax. Try and come up with at least ten things and have it close at hand whenever you need it. I don't have to mention that food isn't allowed do I?

_____

_____

_____

_____

_____

_____

_____

_____

_____

TIP Manage your stress. Make time each day for relaxation. Whenever you have the urge to comfort eat, take a look at your list of pleasures and pick something from it. See the chapter on stress for more on stress and its management.

You may want to include exercise on your list of ways to relax. It is a fantastic way to relieve stress and is far better for you than a giant sized bag of chips. The chapter on exercise goes into the importance of exercise to your happiness. **TIP**

TIP Set aside time for your hobby. If you don't have one, then find one. Pursue something you've always wanted to know more about. Make sure to keep things interesting, as hobbies are a great way to give you a flow experience, so any thoughts of food are forgotten. See the chapter Living a Life of Passion.

TIP Know who your support is and know you can call on them when needed. Having someone to talk things over with is important. You can even send them an email to get your feelings out. Even better, find someone who you can talk to when you are craving food – someone you know will not encourage you to just pig out. See the support chapter for more on this.

Develop an internal locus of control. Recognise how **TIP** much control you have over your own life. This includes how you respond to events that are seemingly beyond your control. By taking active control of your life you are able to do things to make it a better one. It can help you recognise that you do have control over your eating. You also have the power to make the necessary changes in your life. See more about locus of control in the chapter on change.

TIP It's easy to turn to food when you've had an argument with someone. Instead, make a plan to make up with them as soon as possible. The chapter on relationship satisfaction discusses how to resolve conflict. You may also want to look at the chapter on forgiveness.

Recognise that you deserve to look after yourself. You **TIP** deserve to get the best from your body and looking after it will bring you these rewards. Food gives you the energy to live your life, allowing you to do the things you want to do. A life so fun-filled there's no time for emotional eating. I discuss body image in the chapter on self-acceptance.

In addition, you might want to consider the following tips:

TIP Get enough sleep. Tiredness may not only lower your resolve, but it can also lead you to eating unhealthy foods. It's easy to justify getting a take-away, declaring you are too tired to cook. You may even end up eating more as you mistake tiredness for hunger. You find yourself eating when really you should be sleeping.

TIP Learn how to problem solve. It's the non-edible way of dealing with your concerns. To distance yourself emotionally from your problem, put pen to paper. Write down your problem and brainstorm as many potential solutions as possible. Get creative and discard nothing, as one seemingly daft idea may lead on to something great. Then work through each possible solution and write down the pros and cons for each. From this you should be able to come up with a workable solution. Work out the details of the solution and then remember to apply it.

TIP Set a rule that nothing will be eaten in front of the television. After a stressful day, it is easy to curl up in front of the TV, mindlessly eating. Instead, just focus on your programme. If you want to eat, make yourself get up and eat elsewhere. Then focus on the food, without distraction. Take your time and relish (no pun intended) the flavours and textures.

Chapter 25

ONWARDS: WHERE TO GO FROM HERE

Hopefully by now you have touched on different areas of your life in an attempt to promote happiness. Life can get busy, but I hope you will find the time for laughter, relaxation and to indulge in your all-important passion.

Do you understand a bit more about what it means to be happy? Revisit your definition at the start of the book. Has it changed at all?

_____

_____

_____

_____

_____

_____

Have your happiness levels changed at all? In what way? Were there any areas of your life that have particularly benefitted?

_____

_____

_____

_____

_____

_____

Was there a particular topic that made a particular impact on your life?

_____

_____

_____

_____

_____

Which areas do you feel you need further work on?

_____

_____

_____

_____

_____

_____

Going onwards, if you take the skills you have learnt with you, you are giving yourself the best chance of being happy. I can't tell you what will happen in the future. Nobody can. So don't waste your money on so-called fortune tellers. Instead, work on your goals, welcome change and craft a future that is all your own.

Appendix

1 Research support for the health benefits of happiness

2 Goal setting action plan worksheet

3 Barriers and solutions

4 Recommended reading

RESEARCH SUPPORT FOR THE HEALTH BENEFITS OF HAPPINESS

Optimism reduces your risk of dying from heart disease. 1

Optimistic people may live longer. 1

Laughter increases blood vessel function which can reduce the risk of cardiovascular disease. 2

Overall physical health improves when you are optimistic about the future. 1

An optimistic outlook reduces depression. 1

Happiness reduces stress, which is a major cause of many health problems. 1

Happy people may have stronger immune systems and fewer illnesses. 1

Happy people have lower cortisol levels – a hormone associated with stress and ill-health. 3

The happier you are, the less likely you are to have hypertension. 1

Happy people are less likely to suffer from burnout. 1

1 Lyubomirsky et al review 225 studies. See: Lyubomirsky, S., King, L. A., & Diener, E. (2005) The Benefits of Frequent Positive Affect: Does Happiness Lead to Success? *Psychological Bulletin, 131,* 803-855.

2 Laughter is good for your heart, according to a new University of Maryland Medical Center study (2005). Retrieved 16 November 2009 from:

http://www.umm.edu/news/releases/laughter.htm

3 Steptoe, A.P.A., Wardle, J., Marmot, M. (2005). Positive affect and health-related neuroendocrine, cardiovascular and inflammatory processes. *Proceedings of the National Academy of Sciences of the United States of America* 102, 6508-6512. ISSN: 0027-8424

GOAL SETTING ACTION PLAN

Goal:

Steps to be taken	When step is to be actioned

BARRIERS AND SOLUTIONS

Goal:

Potential barriers	Proposed solutions

RECOMMENDED READING

As well as the book suggestions I've offered throughout this workbook, you might also like to consider the following:

Learned Optimism by Martin Seligman.

Authentic Happiness by Martin Seligman.

Man's Search for Meaning by Victor E Frankl.

Any book from the world of positive psychology, including works by Tal Ben-Shaher, Ed Diener, Barbara Fredrickson and Sonja Lyubomirsky.

Any book that enhances your pleasure in the things you enjoy, or are curious to know more about.

INDEX

www.ingramcontent.com/pod-product-compliance
Lightning Source LLC
Chambersburg PA
CBHW060924040426
42445CB00011B/781